A gift for:
Tonya
Be blessed!

From:
Linda Crosby
1 COR 13

Laughing in the Midst of Marriage

Finding Joy in Being a Wife

Linda Ann Crosby

© 2009 by Linda Ann Crosby

Published by Randall House
114 Bush Road
Nashville, TN 37217

All rights reserved. No portion of this publication may be reproduced, stored in a retrieval system, or transmitted in any form or by any means—electronic, mechanical, photocopy, recording, or any other means—except for brief quotation in critical reviews, without the prior written permission of the publisher.

All Scripture quotations, unless otherwise indicated, are taken from The New International Version of the Bible (NIV) © 1984 by the International Bible Society. Used by permission of Zondervan Bible Publishers. Other Scripture references are from the following sources: The New King James Version (NKJV) © 1979, 1980, 1982, 1992, 2005 Thomas Nelson, Inc., Publisher and are used by permission and The Holy Bible, King James Version (KJV).

Printed in the United States of America

ISBN 13: 9780892655779

To my parents,
Ed and Grace Nikander,
who have shared 50+ years of marriage
demonstrating love, joy and commitment.

Dad and Mom were my first example of
laughing in the midst of marriage.
I have fond memories of annual anniversary
dinners, thousands of deeds of service
and love notes on the coffee pot.

Table of Contents

For Better or Worse
Master Videographers 2
Family Foto Shoot 4
Chocolate Caboose 6
It's a Guy Thing 8
'Til the Cows Come Home 10
Fabricated Falsehoods 12
Ministikwin Lake 14
Rock Solid 16
How to Stay Married (by Rick Crosby) 18
Rickey-O Andretti Driving School 20
Pew Sitting 22
My Fairy Tale 24
The Signs of Life 26

For Richer or Poorer
The Pant Peddler 28
Free Hitch, Call 1-800-CROSBYS 30
Treasures Laid Up on Earth 32
Chainsaw Massacre 34
Just Add Water 36
The Seaside Shakedown 38
Wanna Buy a Piece of Junk? 40
Let the Good Times Roll 42
Big Dreams and a Big God 44
Mr. Economical 46
Canadian Coins 48
Frugality at Its Finest 50
Spreading Goodwill 52

In Sickness and Health
Wound-Sucking Machine 54
Sick Bay—No Way! 56
The Hairy, Thirsty Man 58
Never Underestimate the Value of a Wife! 60
Selective Hearing 62
Hats Off to Florence and Clara 64
The Invisible Invalid 66
How to Eat Fresh Worms 68
The Best Medicine 70
Pre-Book-Signing Nightmare 72
Scheduling Conflicts 74
Do You Really Want to Hurt Me? 76
The Midnight Phone Call 78

To Love and To Cherish
Turban or Feather? 80
Dairy Queen Departures 82
The Blue Flower Book 84
Roadway Glamour Shots 86
Wanted: Moving Boxes 88
Great Expectations 90
Call Me Little Red 92
Marital Advice x 2 94
It All Comes Out in the Wash 96
Sunglasses and Lipstick 98
A Woman's Place Is in the Laundry Room 100
All Hail Houdini 102
A Wife's Alphabet 104

introduction

It was May 1987 when Rick and I pledged our love and lives together as two young and dumb kids with big dreams. But God saw who He brought together and said, "It is good." I'm sure He did! The Lord Jesus has been our faithful God as we have held onto each other, while experiencing every rich, poor, sick, healthy, better and worse vow we promised each other with starry eyes over 22 years ago. It has not always been easy. It has not always been fun. But God is faithful, and we're staying married "'til death do us part."

Luke 12:48b states, "From everyone who has been given much, much will be demanded; and from the one who has been entrusted with much, much more will be asked." We have been given much more than our fair share of life and marriage experiences—for the sake of learning and laughing together, and for sharing what we've lived through with others—all for the glory of God.

May you laugh, cry and relate to these stories as you wander down the winding path of our marriage with us. My prayer is that you will be encouraged to see the brighter side of sweet, righteous monogamy! Let loose and laugh at what God has brought you through together.

Linda Ann Crosby

> *For this reason a man will leave his father and mother and be united to his wife, and the two will become one flesh. So they are no longer two, but one. Therefore what God has joined together, let man not separate.*
> Mark 10:7-9

For Better or Worse

Master Videographers

> *My dear brothers, take note of this: Everyone should be quick to listen, slow to speak and slow to become angry, for man's anger does not bring about the righteous life that God desires.*
>
> James 1:19–20
>
> *Do not make friends with a hot-tempered man, do not associate with one easily angered, or you may learn his ways and get yourself ensnared.*
>
> Proverbs 22:24–25

The first fateful, lame videographer outing was whale watching. Within 20 minutes of being on the boat, the captain spotted a beauty and we followed her for two hours. Incredible! Fortunately, Rick was videotaping the entire thrill-of-a-lifetime so we could relive the sighting over and over. Not so, as it turned out. The sun was brightly shining, making it difficult to read the teeny, lit words in the eyepiece of the camera. Somehow Rick, Master Videographer, got PAUSE confused with PLAY . . . for the entire Gray Whale sighting. However, we do have lots of footage, but the whale never made an appearance. There are at least 45 minutes of Rick's shoes, as he held the camera in front of himself. Multiple times you hear the Captain on the intercom saying, "She's just off the bow. She is getting ready to surface. Here she comes . . . here she comes. . . ." And just when the milky back of the whale is slightly visible under the water, the video camera shuts off—until the whale has again plunged beneath the surface, and Rick's shoes return. I'm telling you, it was comical.

The second fateful, lame videographer outing was the Ace Bailey's Hockey Skills competition in New York. I was the one responsible for the video footage of our son, Austin, receiving the Fastest Skater in the USA Award from a New York Rangers NHL player. I had PLAY and PAUSE figured out. What I missed was removing the lens cap, held securely in its place on the front of the camera. So we do actually have a sound recording of the presentation, but then you hear me whine loudly, "Ooooooh Nooooooo!" That's when the picture appears and all is well, just tardy.

When we watched each of these videos for the first time in the hotel room, I couldn't even see the screen for the tears blurring my vision from laughing so hard. Thank the good Lord we had the camera both times, so we'll at least have pictures to look at of a spouting whale and the fastest 10-year-old in America.

Both of these situations were honest mistakes that could've easily brought out anger and hostility from the non-offending spouse. Yes, the results were disappointing, but what good would it have done to get mad? Let's aim at being like the Lord, as described in Exodus 34:6: "compassionate and gracious . . . slow to anger, abounding in love and faithfulness." Being a gracious person helps to make the bumps on life's road so much less painful.

Rick and Linda, Master Videographers, are available to record your life's most important moments. Cheap prices with reference to this story. Please call 1-800-WE-R-LAME.

Family Foto Shoot

> *He has made everything beautiful in its time. He has also set eternity in the hearts of men; yet they cannot fathom what God has done from beginning to end. I know that there is nothing better for men than to be happy and do good while they live. That everyone may eat and drink, and find satisfaction in all his toil—this is the gift of God. I know that everything God does will endure forever; nothing can be added to it and nothing taken from it. God does it so that men will revere him.*
>
> Ecclesiastes 3:11–14

Late in November I came up with the brilliant idea to take a family picture for our Christmas card. When the family was clad in white shirts and jeans, we headed off to a park in our neighborhood with my sister-in-law, the stand-in photographer. My theory was if we took 100 pictures, the odds were that we would find one worthy of Christmas card insertion. We sat on boulders. We lined up like a train. We posed like models. We smiled . . . and even tried to be serious. The shutter clicked away, and I left the park with a hopeful heart.

At home I loaded all 96 pictures onto the computer, then onto the Costco photo site and started eliminating bloopers. His eyes are closed. She isn't smiling. He's smiling like the Cheshire cat. Where did that double chin come from? Blowing wind causes Mohawks. Eventually, with voting from all the family, a picture was chosen and I ordered 100 copies.

I was so proud of myself for orchestrating such a successful photo shoot. The chosen snapshot was so cute of everyone. I just had to go to the computer and view my masterpiece once more. When ordering from Costco, the photos you see are small, so I enlarged it to full screen for my viewing pleasure. Seeing the prize picture at 10"x14", I suddenly realized something was amiss. Behind us were trees with large posts staking them to reduce tumbling. There were only six stakes all together in the park, but seven showed up behind us. I zoomed in. The seventh one wasn't a post—it was a finger. Oh, good grief! My husband was doing the peace sign (bunny ears) behind our daughter's head . . . AND I HAD JUST ORDERED 100 COPIES!

Immediately I phoned Costco. When the nice lady working the photo machine answered, I blurted out, "I married a dork!" Brilliant, I know. Further explanation confirmed in the lady's mind that it was a dorky move on Rick's part. But she reassured me that the order could be halted, and I could choose an appropriate substitute in which Mr. Prankster was not revealing his true colors.

Four hours elapsed from the dork phone call to when I finally laughed about the bunny ears. Once again, I realized it was Rick's keen sense of humor that drew me to him, just like a fly to fly paper. I was stuck, and truly happy for the joy he brings to our marriage. Ecclesiastes 3:12 states, "I know that there is nothing better for men than to be happy and do good while they live." Well, Rick is happy. I'm not too sure about the "do good" part, however.

CHOCOLATE CABOOSE

> *A quarrelsome wife is like a constant dripping on a rainy day; restraining her is like restraining the wind or grasping oil with the hand. As iron sharpens iron, so one man sharpens another. He who tends a fig tree will eat its fruit, and he who looks after his master will be honored. As water reflects a face, so a man's heart reflects the man.*
>
> Proverbs 27:15–19

Rick and I were asked to speak at a couple's night at our church. The topic chosen was "Differences," and we were asked to share how we've melded together to stay in wedded bliss. Initially, when we shared our life histories together, it seemed the differences were few and the similarities numerous. However, the longer we've been married the more the opposite has proven to be true. Rick and I planned to banter back and forth about our likes and dislikes: basketball versus hockey, action movies versus chick flicks, Ranch-flavored Doritos versus plain Doritos, Elvis' Christmas tunes versus all the other Christmas music in the universe. You get the picture.

Before we began, the pastor told everyone they had three minutes to get some dessert and then we would begin. To my surprise, Rick traipsed back to the dessert table and picked out a delicious-looking piece of chocolate cream pie, topped with whipped cream piled a mile high. He returned to the front of the sanctuary and I inquired, "When do you plan to eat that? It's time for us to start." "Oh, yeah," he realized and placed the pie on a chair nearby. Just then the pastor grabbed the microphone to introduce us, so being courteous, Rick sat down . . . ON the chocolate cream pie topped with the mile-high mountain of whipped cream. Of course, he was sporting black jeans, so every little drop of creamy sweetness showed up strikingly on his black backside. After the pastor presented "Rick and Linda Crosby," Rick went to the mic with the pie still hanging from his Levi's and announced, "There will be a delay here while my wife wipes my bum." And I did—in front of everyone—being the compassionate (laundry doing) wife that I am. I figured the more of the sticky mess I got off his pants right then, the less I would have to get out later!

To me, the go-get-the-pie-before-speaking story glaringly broadcasted one of the many differences between us. Rick goes with the flow without thinking past the moment at hand. I am forever guessing what will happen next and how I might improve it. Being married to Rick has pulled me from the fast lane to the middle lane. Likewise, Rick has steered from the slow lane to the middle lane where we've joined forces. Both of us needed a speed adjustment in order to reach out to more people than we could individually. God uses marriage as the tool to rub off our rough edges and make us more like Him. "As iron sharpens iron, so one man sharpens another" (Proverbs 27:17). Does your marriage need some sharpening?

it's a guy thing

> *The God of Israel spoke, the Rock of Israel said to [David]: "When one rules over men in righteousness, when he rules in the fear of God, he is like the light of morning at sunrise on a cloudless morning, like the brightness after rain that brings the grass from the earth." . . . [David said,] "But evil men are all to be cast aside like thorns, which are not gathered with the hand. Whoever touches thorns uses a tool of iron or the shaft of a spear; they are burned up where they lie."*
>
> 2 Samuel 23:3–4, 6–7

Let me take you back to a cool, cloudless day in the city of Phoenix, where a family hike was under way. There was no path, simply a rocky hill with a summit to be conquered. Enter the Teddy Bear cactus. (Sinister music should be playing in the background here.) Numerous times we had instructed the kids to leave a wide path between themselves and cacti. Rumor has it that this breed actually reacts to ground movements and can shoot a limb at a passerby. I did not believe it until that fateful day.

We were half way up the incline when my husband yelled, "OOOOUUUUCCCCHHH!" He held up his hand to reveal a Teddy Bear arm embedded in the side of his hand. My insides did the roller-coaster flip-flop upon first glance. "Find something to pull it out!" Rick commanded. Two water bottles were the best retraction devices I could come up with, and I advanced toward the victim. "Wait a minute," he said, stopping me in my tracks. Rick searched his pockets with his "good" hand. "I should take a picture of this with my cell phone," he explained. Now, when I'm in pain with a parasite digging its spines into my flesh, I do not think, *Let me take a picture of this!* It has got to be a guy thing.

Photo-shoot behind us, I advanced once more and, on the count of three, I squeezed the bottles against the cactus-laden arm. It dislodged . . . and flew into my thigh. Stuck through my jeans, and secured its new territory wholeheartedly. My eyes bulged from my head, and I believe my heart stopped momentarily. Confirming what I had earlier surmised, I did not once think of taking a picture of my pain. I'm such a girl.

When I gained mental fortitude, I squeezed the bottles once again and I was indeed cactus free. Later that night, simply for the comparison factor, we counted blood-dot entry points. Rick's hand had nine. Linda's leg had 23. I won, but I don't have a picture on my phone to show for it.

I believe God put men at the head of the marriage to rule in the fear of God, because they respond so bravely when they're in pain. Rick remained cool and collected with spines digging in his hand. I could not have told you what my name was while that cactus was stuck in my leg. I lost sight of reality and was unable to focus when calamity hit. Rick's sense of humor remained intact even during the agony. God knew it was a guy thing, and He put the less emotional person in charge for times of trials. I, for one, am so glad He did.

'TiL THE COWS COME HOME

> *Surely God is my salvation; I will trust and not be afraid. The LORD, the LORD, is my strength and my song; he has become my salvation. With joy you will draw water from the wells of salvation. In that day you will say: "Give thanks to the LORD, call on his name; make known among the nations what he has done, and proclaim that his name is exalted."*
>
> Isaiah 12:2–4

The year was 1985 when Rick took me home to Wildwood, Alberta to meet the parents . . . and the six siblings, the dog, the horse and the chickens. Rick's dad was the pastor in the little town, and the PK (preacher's kid) was taking me to his church for the first time. On our way, we were approaching a neighbor's farm when Rick announced, "The Hermann's cows are out. We'd better stop and put them back in." His *"we"* was used in the loosest sense of that word since there were merely two of us in the vehicle, and one was NOT helping put cows back in while wearing her Sunday best and high heels.

It's beyond me how Rick sweet-talked me into assisting him that day, but he did. He persuaded me to stand in the middle of the dirt road with my arms spread wide, so the cows would turn into the farmyard and not go beyond the impressive, physical barrier I was to provide. I was not in familiar territory, to say the absolute least. Terrifyingly, I was left alone by the wide-open gate, while Rick jogged back down the road to jump-start the stampede. These were not ordinary Jersey cows. Nooooooo!

These were their Amazon cousins from the Limousin family, standing taller than me and outweighing me by 800 pounds each.

Cow chasing commenced. Imagine me trembling from head to toe, holding wobbly arms out in a half-bent fashion, prepared to hit the dirt in the fetal position at any second. Rick had the bovine indeed stampeding. To my utter amazement, the plan worked like a charm. The beasts approached, turned on a dime, trotted into their pasture, did an about-face and looked at me, probably wondering, *Where did that wimpy city-slicker come from?*

When we arrived at the church all sparkling clean with no sign of cow on us, I was still shaky and must have looked like the most feeble, frightened little waif Rick had ever brought to church.

Many times in our marriage I've had to trust Rick beyond what was comfortable for me. Because of placing more and more trust in Rick over the years, my faith in him has grown—tremendously. One of my challenges early on was transferring my father's protection of me to my husband. When Rick suggested going camping, I couldn't imagine going without Dad. Who would take care of me??? Oh yeah, you . . . and the Lord.

That same principle applies in our relationship with the Lord; the more trust we put in Him, the more we rely on His care and comfort. Is there something bigger than you stampeding your way? Hand it over to Jesus, the one whose arms were spread wide when He died for you.

Fabricated Falsehoods

> *When we put bits into the mouths of horses to make them obey us, we can turn the whole animal. Or take ships as an example. Although they are so large and are driven by strong winds, they are steered by a very small rudder wherever the pilot wants to go. Likewise the tongue is a small part of the body, but it makes great boasts. Consider what a great forest is set on fire by a small spark. The tongue also is a fire, a world of evil among the parts of the body. . . . Out of the same mouth come praise and cursing. My brothers, this should not be.*
>
> James 3:3–6a, 10

OK, I'll admit that I'm gullible. I believe people. Why would people lie? "Do unto others" and all that jazz. Looking back at the "little white lies" I've fallen for, I can see that I was an easy target for a prankster, a huckster, a foolhardy numbskull, a liar—Rick. Strap on your seatbelts as we venture together down the slippery slope of untruths my soon-to-be-husband spewed upon me. (He has since repented, by the way.)

First he confessed, half embarrassed, that he could not whistle. For a good week or so, I painstakingly gave whistling lessons to the poor chap. We were in line at the TWU café one evening and Rick actually whistled! I was overjoyed and proud of my pupil. I congratulated him profusely . . . then I noticed everyone around us was laughing hysterically—at me. Come to find out, Rick was thoroughly captivated with my puckering demonstrations. Whatever.

Rick is of First Nations ancestry, which is the politically correct way to say he's an Indian. Previously in college, I had studied Native Americans and felt I had some grasp of their ways. So when Rick explained that his Indian grandmother had christened him with a native name, I believed him. It only took me a day or two to contemplate the peculiar name and realize how ridiculous it was: Chief Running Beaver Meat. Whatever.

In the last college hockey game before Christmas break, Rick took a puck to the mouth. One of his front teeth cracked three times straight across. Rick went home to Alberta and I to California. Many phone calls kept us in touch during the holidays. During one of those calls, Rick dismayingly reported that he had to get his cracked tooth capped and that the new one didn't match in color or shape. I was imagining a big Billy-Bob bucked tooth that stuck out like a brown two-by-four in a white picket fence. Lo and behold, the whole capped tooth story was a falsehood. He still has the tooth with triplicate cracks. Whatever.

Rick's jesting was done in fun, but quite often in marriage lying occurs in order to smooth things over. The tongue is the most powerful muscle we must learn to control. In James 3 the tongue is seen like: a bit and a rudder with the power to direct; a fire that can heat things up and even destroy; animals that are dangerous and poisonous; salt water and a fig tree with the power to delight. Without the Holy Spirit working in us, our tongues can be dangerous weapons against a strong marriage. Proverbs 15:4 says, "The tongue that brings healing is a tree of life, but a deceitful tongue crushes the spirit." Bring healing to your marriage by being honest and truthful.

Ministikwin Lake

> *You were taught, with regard to your former way of life, to put off your old self, which is being corrupted by its deceitful desires; to be made new in the attitude of your minds; and to put on the new self, created to be like God in true righteousness and holiness.... "In your anger do not sin": Do not let the sun go down while you are still angry, and do not give the devil a foothold.*
>
> Ephesians 4:22–24, 26–27

Accepting change is not easy for me, especially when it involves something I do not want to do. It was the Christmas season of 2004, and my sister's family had arrived to spend three weeks in Phoenix with the rest of our family. They only visit us every other year, so all of us, particularly the nine grandkids, were looking forward to games and food and fun. About a week before Christmas, my dear husband told me that he had a Boxing Day surprise for me. (Boxing Day is a Canadian holiday observed on December 26th.) Anticipation and glee pervaded my heart. I *love* surprises! Not knowing makes my mind go *wild* with wonder, and it simply causes life to be extra exhilarating for me.

That was all blown to bits later, though, when he told me my surprise: a family road trip to Ministikwin Lake, Saskatchewan—an 1890 mile *one-way* trip straight north from Phoenix to Canada's frozen tundra. Rick's parents had rented a teeny log cabin on the frozen-solid lake, and his brother's family was also going. Now, Crosby family get-togethers are filled with fun, laughter and frivolity, but keep in mind it was December. AND MY SISTER'S FAMILY WAS VISITING!

I'd like to report that I smiled and said, "Sure, honey!" but it didn't go down that smoothly between us. In fact, there were several lively discussions behind closed doors. With tears flooding my eyes, I found my carefully prepared Christmas list, crossed off everything, wrote PARKA in big letters then handed it to Rick. (This was the 'accepting change' part of the story.)

We drove for three days through rain, sleet, and even snow to a 700-square-foot cabin where 13 of us were stuffed in for a week. It was cozy, to say the absolute least. Did I forget to mention that it was *minus fifty degrees*? A "rink" was cleared on the lake, and the men and kids were captivated with hockey the entire week. I did a puzzle.

The moral of this story is: When life hands you snow make snowballs and annihilate your opponent. It truly does make you feel better. Truthfully, incomparable family memories were made, and I got a warm, black parka out of the deal.

You may ask, how did this impact your life? Well, we're still married. The forced trek north did go down in the family history books as the maddest I've ever been, but like I said, we're still *happily* married. Sometimes you just have to give in and do what you *don't* want to do to keep the peace. It's like my momma used to say, "Do something you don't want to do every day. It makes you a better person."

ROCK SOLID

> *Joshua called together the twelve men he had appointed from the Israelites, one from each tribe, and said to them, "Go over before the ark of the Lord your God into the middle of the Jordan. Each of you is to take up a stone on his shoulder . . . to serve as a sign among you. In the future when your children ask you, 'What do these stones mean?' Tell them that the flow of the Jordan was cut off before the ark of the covenant of the Lord. When it crossed the Jordan, the waters of the Jordan were cut off. These stones are to be a memorial to the people of Israel forever."*
>
> Joshua 4:4–7

One evening my husband casually mentioned that some cutbacks were announced at his place of employment. There were four pilots and two airplanes, and one plane was going to be sold. Having passed math in first grade, I deduced that two pilots would be looking for new employment. Rick had been the last one hired, so his chances looked slim.

Rick had been flying with that company for just shy of one year, and I rather liked the fact that he was home in time for dinner. That was unusual for a pilot position. It's just sooooo like God to stir up your life when you are comfortable, and not really relying on Him.

The day following my husband's announcement, I basically freaked out. Most women can relate to being emotionally out of control: spontaneous crying brought on by disconnected thoughts, anger at no one in particular and an unnatural favor to your children, as you picture them living on the street in a cardboard box.

It was mid-afternoon and I was catatonically staring out the kitchen window, while washing the same pot over and over, when something snapped. The thought came to me, *What in the world am I doing pouting like this? We live in America, the most prosperous country in the world. I have three healthy children and a wonderful husband. We have a house, two cars and a blow-up swimming pool. Who am I to worry about tomorrow? The Lord has it all under control.*

Joshua 4:8–9 tells the story of the Israelites picking up twelve stones from the midst of the Jordan. They piled them up as a memorial to when the Lord stopped the river so the Ark of the Covenant could be carried through on dry ground. The rocks were to be a reminder to them of what the Lord had done.

Remembering Joshua and the twelve tribes, I marched out to the backyard. With dish-soapy hands I gathered rocks and piled them by the back fence. The pile went unnoticed by most of my family members. But for the three months from Rick's announcement to the official "letting go" of two pilots, I looked at that heap and thanked the Lord for faithfully providing for us. My faith was strengthened by that mound of stones, and the God of Israel showed Himself miraculously once again, as my husband was one of the two pilots who stayed with the company.

HOW TO STAY MARRIED (BY RICK CROSBY)

> *"Teacher," they said, "Moses told us that if a man dies without having children, his brother must marry the widow and have children for him. Now there were seven brothers among us. The first one married and died, and since he had no children, he left his wife to his brother. The same thing happened to the second and third brother, right on down to the seventh. Finally, the woman died. Now then, at the resurrection, whose wife will she be of the seven, since all of them were married to her?" Jesus replied, "You are in error because you do not know the Scriptures or the power of God. At the resurrection people will neither marry nor be given in marriage; they will be like the angels in heaven."*
>
> Matthew 22:24–30

Most husbands realize there are benefits to complimenting their wives. The problem for some men is, they simply lack the know-how to pull it off without spending a night on the couch.

To remedy this situation and aid his fellow man, my husband has decided to pen a book of helpful hints for husbands. It's actually a list of what not to say to your wife if you plan to stay married. Unfortunately, quite a few entries were born from his own complimentary blunders. Thankfully, though, I know his heart's intention, and I have a sense of humor.

A few of the choice entries from Rick's friends include:

"You're a beauty in disguise."

"I wish my calves were as big as yours."

"Don't worry if the pants I bought are too big for you. You'll grow into them."

"I never noticed before how much facial hair you have." (Ugh!)

My personal favorite occurred as Rick was trying to "speak my language." I was an art major when we met and took several art classes during our first years of marriage. Rick climbed into bed one night and amorously purred, "Lin, you're more beautiful than the women Leonardo da Vinci painted." Laughter exploded from inside of me, completely confusing Rick. I scrambled to get my *History of Art* book and proceeded to show Casanova several of the roly-poly, pudgy women that Leo had painted. For his defense he replied, "See, I told you that you were more beautiful!"

Matthew 22:30 comes to my mind. It states that, at the resurrection, we won't be married. We will be like angels. Obviously being an angel and being married are *different,* as proven by "husbandly" compliments. It would benefit all of us if we acted in more angelic ways when it comes to marriage. Angels hear directly from God and carry out His will. Angels defend the weak and protect the righteous. Angels do most of their work unnoticed. And angels rejoice every single time someone turns their life over to the Lord.

Every once in a long while, Rick endearingly calls me Angel-face. That name alone cancels out several of his other "compliments."

Men. Ya gotta love 'em.

Rickey-O Andretti Driving School

> *He who finds a wife finds what is good and receives favor from the LORD. . . . A quarrelsome wife is like a constant dripping. Houses and wealth are inherited from parents, but a prudent wife is from the LORD.*
>
> Proverbs 18:22; 19:13b–14

My husband claims he did not know he was strong-willed until we were engaged to be married. That's hard to believe from a 20-year-old male who played various sports and grew up with six siblings. Rick alleges the fortress within him was birthed in his car on Highway 280 in California with me by his side. Au contraire. That was simply the day the giant was awakened.

Country driving comprised most of Rick's road experience. He learned to drive on Frog Alley in Wildwood, Alberta—not exactly a metropolis. Needless to say, it was apparent to me that Rick's driving habits would require some expertise on my part when in my territory, the sunshine state. A shoulder check in California occurs within a nanosecond. In the time that elapsed while my sweet fiancé ensured that his blind spot was indeed vacant, I could shampoo, lather, rinse, repeat.

Out of all the men in the world, I picked Rick, partly due to his even temper, mild manner and calm reserve. Who knew that deep in the recesses of his heart there was a warrior waiting to conquer a maiden? And who knew I was the maiden?

The climax of our driving dilemma materialized while navigating rush-hour traffic in San Jose. Rick was requiring a high amount of assistance and, thankfully, I was there for him. He, however, considered my help verbal harassment. Warrior-Man arose, stealthily in his own stubborn way. Rick s-h-o-u-l-d-e-r c-h-e-c-k-e-d, signaled, and drove off Highway 280. When the car rolled to a halt, Rick exited fully composed. After marching around to my side he half-yelled, half-barked at my rolled-up window, "Get out! You drive!" I swiftly reached up and locked my door. Sweet mercy, if he wanted me to be quiet he could've just said so.

Thankfully, when the steam venting from his ears subsided, he resumed command of the car. The days of saving my life while Rick maneuvered on the fast-paced highways of California were over. From then on I was at the mercy of this country boy and his skill behind the wheel. God help him.

What I failed to realize was, Rick had been driving for six years in his little, country town. Surprisingly, husbands come to marriage with quite a few skills previously mastered. A well-meaning, blabber-mouth wife is not the prize our husbands were hoping for when they read in Proverbs that finding a wife is a good deal. Seriously, sometimes we need to leave well enough alone!

pew sitting

> *Let us hold unswervingly to the hope we profess, for he who promised is faithful. And let us consider how we may spur one another on toward love and good deeds. Let us not give up meeting together, as some are in the habit of doing, but let us encourage one another—and all the more as you see the Day approaching.*
>
> Hebrews 10:23–25

The year was 1999. We were looking for a new family-oriented church, not too huge, where we could feel like we belonged. Friends of ours invited us to a church that was just opening up, so we packed up the children and checked it out. My husband, Rick, loved it immediately. He loved the preaching. He loved the worship music. He loved all the new people with whom he could talk. On our second Sunday, Rick jumped into serving, donning a purple polo shirt on parking-lot patrol.

I didn't resist the change of going to a new church; I just didn't think *this* was the church for us. I sat unhappily in the pew for 18 months, feeling like I didn't belong. Rick kept encouraging me to go in order to set a good example for our three kids. So I went. I heard the sermons. I was awed by the musicians. I saw lots of new faces. But I didn't get involved at all. My heart was kept in a tight little box, protected from becoming exposed and vulnerable.

Once I apologized to God and Rick, I began to realize all that I was missing at our chosen place of worship. After a year and a half I followed Rick's example, finally stepping out of my comfort zone to meet people and make friends. I even started a "Martha Stewart" decorating, cooking and crafting class for women (minus Martha, of course).

Admittedly, I was burned out from overwork and frustration in a previous church, but until I realized that I was the one who had to decide to smarten up, my attitude was pretty awful. That ol' hindsight saying came nipping at my heels yet again. Why did it take me so long? I don't know . . . maybe selfish pride. What did I lose? Eighteen months of spiritual growth and untold friendships that slipped between my fingers that were firmly folded in my lap.

We've now been at 'our' church for over ten years, and we love the fellowship, the truth from the Word and the lifelong friendships we have made.

Are you miserable in your church? I've been there, done that, wrote the story. Here's my advice: Decide to be a blessing and find somewhere and someone to serve. Look for opportunities in the nursery, the flower bed, the choir or in an outreach ministry. You won't be satisfied if you stay on the receiving end in your church.

My Fairy Tale

> *A cheerful look brings joy to the heart, and good news gives health to the bones. . . . To man belong the plans of the heart, but from the LORD come the reply of the tongue. All a man's ways seem innocent to him, but motives are weighed by the LORD. Commit to the LORD whatever you do, and your plans will succeed.*
>
> Proverbs 15:30; 16:1–3

I married my knight in shining armor years ago. He rode up on his ivory colt (Dodge Colt), swept me off my feet and rescued me from a life as a mere princess to be his queen. We enjoyed ruling our kingdom together. A few servants would have been a good thing, but life was heading toward happily ever after without hired help.

Once our royal family was graced with the princess and two princes, my fairytale was starting to get foggy. My crown was tarnished because I never had any time to myself to work on me. My castle was cramped with a crib, changing table, high chair, bouncy seat, swing and colossal plastic toys. I knew the situation was a season in our lives, but I felt like the Beauty who needed rescuing once again.

When Rick finished flying each day, he would call to announce that his return to the castle would be in thirty minutes. I valued this time to apply some of the beauty secrets that Queen Esther used (see Esther 2:12). More often than not, I felt like I needed Esther's "six months with oil of myrrh and six with perfumes and cosmetics," but I constructively used a few minutes to look my best. My cover was blown one evening as my little princess announced at the dinner table, "Dad, Mommy puts on her lick-stick and makeup right before you open the door." I wanted to throw her in the dungeon.

Before my knight crosses the moat, sautéing onions is an illusion that I use regularly. Rick's half-hour warning call catches me off-guard some days, and sends me scrambling through the cupboards and freezer for dinner ideas. He usually spends time unwinding and playing with the kids, giving me a few moments to cook. But I want him to savor an inviting aroma when he graces our threshold, so before my knight arrives, I slice and dice an onion and sauté it in butter. He believes I'm preparing a culinary delight, and I believe I have time to throw one together while the onions sizzle in the pan.

My husband also appreciates a clean castle to welcome him after a long day of slaying giants and fighting dragons down at the airport. Some days it seems impossible. My goal each evening is to tidy the rooms that are visible from the front door. Illusions can be a good thing.

The Signs of Life

> *Enter through the narrow gate. For wide is the gate and broad is the road that leads to destruction, and many enter through it. But small is the gate and narrow the road that leads to life, and only a few find it.*
>
> Matthew 7:13–14

Being a sensible, educated woman, I read any and all printed material in the scope of my vision while driving or riding in a vehicle. Heaven knows the information had to be important if someone paid to put it on a billboard. Little did I realize that my helpfulness was creating a driving deficit for my man. I'm not sure if he tuned me out, or depended on the volume of my reading to increase if action were truly required of him. Anyway, it came to my attention that Rick no longer read the highway signs. Or any sign for that matter. None. At all.

During our first years of marriage, we relocated from Vancouver, B.C. to northern Alberta, a 24-hour drive. At the helm in a borrowed pickup truck, pulling a U-Haul trailer stuffed with our worldly plunder, Rick led his young bride to a new frontier. Submissively, I brought up the rear in our VW Rabbit.

For those who are unfamiliar with Canadian terrain, let me explain something fundamental regarding the roadways. There is one major highway running East and West in Canada. It is Highway One. In most of the western provinces, there is only one major highway bearing North-South. Pretty simple. In order to navigate our move, there was merely a single exit to be taken during the entire 24 hours. As we approached the designated off ramp, I was chanting, "Come on. Come on. Come on." As the sign and ramp flew by I changed gears to, "Say it isn't so. Say it isn't so." Yep, Rick missed it.

Realizing that I was entirely to blame for his lack of sign reading, I emerged from behind the orange trailer and gunned the Rabbit. Pulling in front of Rick, I signaled, veered onto the shoulder and came to a stop in a cloud of brown dust. He followed suit as would any good captain witnessing a mutiny.

"Why are you pulling over?" *Relax, cowboy.* "You missed the turn," was all I offered. "Oh," was his grandiose retort and we were back on the road again, soon heading north.

Little communication transpired the remainder of the pit stops, but that day I made a solemn vow in the sticky silence: I, Linda Ann Crosby, before God and man, would no longer read signs aloud. Thank the good Lord that Rick reads the Bible and knows about the narrow road leading to life. Only a few find it.

For Richer or Poorer

The Pant Peddler

> *Consider how the lilies grow. They do not labor or spin. Yet I tell you, not even Solomon in all his splendor was dressed like one of these. If that is how God clothes the grass of the field, which is here today, and tomorrow is thrown into the fire, how much more will he clothe you, O you of little faith!*
>
> Luke 12:27–28

Minding our own business at a roadside gas station, Rick and I were stretching our legs on a hazy afternoon while on our way to California. It was a splurge for us to be leaving for the weekend because we had recently relocated from Canada to Phoenix. Rick was in the process of switching over his pilot licenses and wasn't employed yet. We were living off of the equity from the sale of our home and praying hard for a flying job for Rick. Money was tighter than Superman's suit. During the drive we had discussed Rick's need for some dress pants for employment interviews. One pair maximum was all we could afford.

We were standing off to the side of the gas station parking lot when a stranger approached us. His trimmed brown hair and clean shaven chin didn't exactly coincide with his long, orange board shorts, loose fitting tank and worn flip-flops. Looking at my husband he inquired, "Hey, do you wear size 36 x 32 pants?"

"Yeeaaaah," was Rick's drawn out Am-I-on-Candid-Camera reply.

"I have five pair for sale if you want to take a look," he offered as he opened the garment bag he was holding. "Twenty dollars for all of 'em." They were pressed and still hanging on the dry cleaner's hangers.

Long story short, the guy was a laid-off salesman from Los Angeles who was heading to Phoenix, hence the plethora of designer slacks that wondrously "happened" to be Rick's size. The stranger needed gas money and my husband needed dress pants, so the transaction was sealed.

It didn't actually go that smoothly, however, for even though I believe in miracles, I'm highly suspicious of homeless people selling pants at gas stations. While Rick analyzed the pants, I was conducting an inquisition on the pant peddler.

"So you were just waiting outside the gas station for some guy who looked like your size who might want to buy your pants?" I doubtfully asked.

"Yep." He was doing well with full eye contact and no shiftiness that I could detect.

"Where did you get these pants?" I drilled.

"Most of them at Nordstrom's," he offered without hesitating.

Finally satisfied that the guy was legit, I recognized God's hand at work. With a softer tone I asked, "Are you a Christian?"

A smile crossed his face. "Yes, I am. Are you guys?"

"Yes, we are," Rick and I parroted in unison. We discovered that we attended sister churches, and we marveled at God's care and timing to put his children together to meet each of their needs. God is so awesome!

Free Hitch, Call 1-800-Crosbys

> *When Pharaoh let the [Israelites] go, God did not lead them on the road through the Philistine country, though that was shorter. . . . God led the people around by the desert road toward the Red Sea. . . . By day the LORD went ahead of them in a pillar of cloud to guide them on their way and by night in a pillar of fire to give them light, so that they could travel by day or night. Neither the pillar of cloud by day nor the pillar of fire by night left its place in front of the people.*
>
> Exodus 13:17–18, 21–22

Twelve. The number surprised me so I recounted. We had moved twelve times in the first eighteen years of our marriage. Moving is neither convenient nor comfortable. Moving means change. It also means cleaning out the tide pools of our home where the goodies have collected, as the waves of life continued to roll.

Cleaning out was getting increasingly harder because collecting soon-to-be-useful items had secretly become my husband's favorite pastime when I wasn't looking. He had been purchasing priceless on-sale and garage-sale trinkets that we just might need someday. Like the in-home putting machine that returns the golf ball. This might seem normal to some, but Rick has only golfed three times in his life (that's once every 14 years), not to mention the malfunctioning ball return mechanism. Or like the hitch to pull the boat we would love to buy to attach to the truck we don't have.

I'm all about rules. So I made a new rule which always begins by announcing that it is a new rule, as if someone is keeping track of all my rules. Anyway, "New Rule: No more buying stuff that we might need someday."

Five of those twelve moves were to new horizons, new states and/or provinces. Uneasiness continually settled around my heart like an unwelcome friend as we embarked on new adventures. Will I find a bosom friend? Will we be welcomed in a Bible-believing church? Will there be people to connect with who are game-playing "laugh-till-you-have-to-run-to-the-bathroom" comrades? Are we really following God's direction for our family?

The Israelites didn't have it so bad, even though their journey sounds quite unorganized when we hear that they "wandered in the wilderness." Following God's presence as a cloud is hardly wandering. Exodus 13:21 reads, "By day the LORD went ahead of them in a pillar of cloud to guide them on their way and by night in a pillar of fire to give them light, so that they could travel by day or night." Talk about clear direction.

Fortunately for believers, we too can have clear direction from the Lord not only about moving, but also about every area of our lives. Matthew 7:7–8 reads, "Ask and it will be given to you; seek and you will find; knock and the door will be opened to you. For everyone who asks receives; he who seeks finds; and to him who knocks, the door will be opened." Be bold—ask for directions.

Treasures Laid Up on Earth

> *Do not store up for yourselves treasures on earth, where moth and rust destroy, and where thieves break in and steal. But store up for yourselves treasures in heaven, where moth and rust do not destroy, and where thieves do not break in and steal. For where your treasure is, there your heart will be also.*
>
> Matthew 6:19–21

The saying, "One man's trash is another man's treasure" should plainly be, "One spouse's trash is the other spouse's treasure." Every marriage seems to contain a collector and a chucker. Rick likes mementoes. So do I, but mine are in my head and a box in my closet. His are in boxes. Lots of boxes. Stacked-in-the-garage-where-my-van-should-be-parked boxes.

Before we moved across the country, I was helping Rick pack his collection of stuff, and I wrote on each of the boxes "Rick's Junk #7," "Rick's Junk #8," etc. I wasn't intentionally calling it garbage, but that's how he interpreted my box labeling. It wounded my husband that I considered his plastic horses from 1972, his huge blue comb from junior high and his magic kit "junk." After taping shut the last box I considerately wrote, "Rick's Quality Paraphernalia." He has other boxes that have not been exhumed since the Dark Ages labeled: "Rick's T-Shirts: too small but too cool to throw away" and "Rick's College Books: he didn't read them then, and he won't read them again—burn if he dies." I could go on and on, but I'll spare you.

Personally, I feel the marriage vows should contain the phrase "In sickness and in health, collecting and removing. . . ." The Lord eventually showed me the deeper meaning behind Rick's amassed possessions. Shockingly, it's all the same reasons that drew Rick to my heart. He loves people and anything they have given him; hence the plastic horses from the Chief of the Indian Band where he lived as a child. He cherishes happy memories like the comb he was given for having "perfect hair" when he was thirteen. He wants to enjoy all that life has to offer, thus the chance to put on a magic show.

Turning annoying behaviors into positive traits not only gets us focused on the virtues of our husbands, it also gives us more of God's perspective. Proverbs 20:5 says, "The purposes of a man's heart are deep waters, but a man [or woman] of understanding draws them out." God designed each of us to specialize in our area of gifts, interests and talents. Spouses are often the gold diggers that need to uncover the buried treasure in their mates.

chainsaw Massacre

> *To man belong the plans of the heart, but from the LORD comes the reply of the tongue. . . . Commit to the LORD whatever you do, and your plans will succeed. . . . In his heart a man plans his course, but the LORD determines his steps. . . . Whoever gives heed to instruction prospers, and blessed is he who trusts in the LORD. . . . Many are the plans in a man's heart, but it is the LORD's purpose that prevails.*
>
> Proverbs 16:1, 3, 9, 20; 19:21

Our first home in Phoenix was on an average size lot yet had 26 mature trees, including two Eucalyptus trees well over 80 feet tall. Those two trees dropped more leaves, seeds and bark into our neighbor's swimming pools than did their own foliage. Loathing all the clean-up required, and being cordial neighbors, the decision was made to take out the larger of the two offending trees from our front yard. After many inquiries to $600 tree-removal services, my thrift-conscious husband rented a chain saw and called in our brother-in-law, Brian, as an accomplice.

Knowing all too well how catastrophic yard maintenance projects had gone in the past (and the number of fence posts that we'd already replaced), I suggested that Rick call our insurance company simply to find out our coverage *if,* for instance, an 80-foot Eucalyptus tree hit our house, the neighbor's house, or our car. Thankfully we had "stupid homeowner chainsaw coverage." Whew.

The plan was priceless. Our home faced a cul-de-sac that was conveniently long enough to accommodate a large tree lying down the middle of the street, if need be. With a large rope coiled over his shoulder, my able-bodied husband climbed 30 feet up the tree and secured the rope. The other end of the rope was tied to the back of our family car. After some quick mental calculations, I hoped and prayed that the rope was longer than the tree was tall.

With safety helmets on their heads, and my children and I safely standing 150 feet down the street, the chainsaw was ripped to a roaring start and prayers were sent heavenward. Brian notched the back of the tree while Rick drove the pull-away car. Amazingly, the plan went down successfully. With a loud thump the tree slammed the pavement precisely where they had hoped and just shy of Rick and the car. Our neighbors came out and cheered, as did I!

Sadly, not all of our plans go this smoothly. Looking back on thwarted business attempts and money-pit car purchases, the times that went awry were when we went ahead without the Lord's direction. Why do we even try to make decisions based on our feeble human feelings? The Lord is ready, willing and able to offer wisdom, advice and peace for every situation. Include God in your marital decisions "and the peace of God, which transcends all understanding, will guard your hearts and your minds in Christ Jesus" (Philippians 4:7).

Just Add Water

> *The LORD will guide you always; he will satisfy your needs in a sun-scorched land and will strengthen your frame. You will be like a well-watered garden, like a spring whose waters never fail. Your people will rebuild the ancient ruins and will raise up the age-old foundations; you will be called Repairer of Broken Walls, Restorer of Streets with Dwellings.*
>
> Isaiah 58:11–12

My husband, whom I love with all my heart, has the fascinating habit of adding water to whatever condiment is getting low on juice: salad dressing, ketchup, BBQ sauce, you name it. Nothing in the door of the fridge is safe. They are all watered down to translucent muck before our eyes. Recently I found out that Rick's dad used to add water. AH HA! Probably still does, too. Nothing bugs me more than cooking a hot dog to perfection on the grill, laying it on a toasted hotdog bun and then dumping pink water on it from the "almost gone" ketchup. Throw the bottle away already!

Rick was sitting at the kitchen table one evening and asked for the ketchup from the kitchen counter. Noticing that it was practically empty, I quickly removed the lid, filled the bottle half full of tap water then replaced the lid. Rick was busily conversing and didn't notice the delay in the requested bottle's delivery to the table. Inside I was secretly hoping he would douse his dog, but unfortunately he has another intriguing habit of shaking the red gooey fluid before opening it. Indeed he noticed the clear consistency where the obliterated tomatoes were supposed to be. "Look!" I pronounced, "We don't need to buy ketchup for another six weeks!" I doubled over in riotous laughter. He did find it semi-amusing . . . then ate the dry wiener in the bun.

Being well watered is not always a bad deal. The last line of Isaiah 58:11 reads, "You will be like a well-watered garden, like a spring whose waters never fail." We originally claimed this verse as our family scripture when we relocated to Arizona, our sun-scorched land. Later I wondered what the well-watered part actually meant. Was the garden watered from a well, or was it a substantially drenched garden? Come to find out, this is a metaphor for love: a well that is continually sending out streams of living water, yet is always full. What a beautiful word picture the Lord prepared for us, not only as Christians, but specifically as wives. It describes the blessing of staying watered by the love of the Lord as we water and nourish our marriages with love—using kind words, lending a helping hand, praising and respecting our husbands. Deep roots of love will not grow into a solid foundation with only occasional watering. Consistency and persistency are needed. Thankfully, the Lord is our source whom we can draw from to water our gardens.

THE seaside shakedown

> When they had finished eating, Jesus said to Simon Peter, "Simon son of John, do you truly love me more than these?" "Yes, Lord," he said, "you know that I love you." Jesus said, "Feed my lambs." Again Jesus said, "Simon son of John, do you truly love me?" He answered, "Yes, Lord, you know that I love you." Jesus said, "Take care of my sheep." The third time he said to him, "Simon son of John, do you love me?" Peter was hurt because Jesus asked him the third time, "Do you love me?" He said, "Lord, you know all things; you know that I love you." Jesus said, "Feed my sheep."
>
> John 21:15–17

Our family escaped to San Diego, California one winter to enjoy the beach and everything God created on the coast. We love to venture off to different touristy spots in the off-season to avoid the crowds and focus on family time. All of us skipped stones and collected shells. We sat on the windy beach for hours and watched the waves roll in. The waves of the sea always remind me of God's love for us. It keeps coming again and again, so faithful no matter what we've done.

What's a stop in San Diego without tasting clam chowder from a restaurant on a pier? Exactly what I was thinking! The five of us crowded into a shiny orange booth at a little fish stand on a chilly night. We tasted different soups, battered fish, and of course fat fries. We laughed and enjoyed each other's company and each one's wind-blown appearance. One child, who got a little overzealous jumping the waves, was wearing a sweatshirt as *pants,* due to very soggy shorts. We were certainly a comical looking bunch.

Upon licking the last tarter-sauced finger, we ventured back onto the pier for a casual stroll. A scruffy-looking man who appeared to be homeless approached my husband and asked for money to buy something to eat. He asked the right guy, that's for sure. Rick has the heart of Jesus and looks for opportunities to "feed His sheep." Leaving the children and me for just a moment, my husband took the man back to the fish stand to order a meal for him. While we were waiting for Rick, another man approached to inform us that the beggar was a fraud and always requested meals from tourists. I thanked the man, and he continued on down the pier. Our kids were aghast that their dad was in the midst of a scam and frantically pleaded for me to put a halt to the heist before his hard-earned money was wasted. I calmly told the kids, "It's not a scam to feed a stranger. We will only be blessed by blessing others." The wheels in their little heads began to spin in understanding.

When Rick returned, the four of us simultaneously explained the situation to him. He got the point and responded, as I knew he would, "Well, he started eating like he was pretty hungry! I'm glad we could help." Often I'm in awe of how kind my husband is to strangers. After 22-plus years of marriage, I still have a boatload of learning to do at his feet.

wanna Buy a piece of junk?

> *The light of the righteous shines brightly, but the lamp of the wicked is snuffed out. Pride only breeds quarrels, but wisdom is found in those who take advice. Dishonest money dwindles away, but he who gathers money little by little makes it grow. Hope deferred makes the heart sick, but a longing fulfilled is a tree of life. He who scorns instruction will pay for it, but he who respects a command is rewarded... Every prudent man acts out of knowledge, but a fool exposes his folly.*
>
> Proverbs 13:9–13, 16

While I was away at a women's retreat in the company of my mother and sister, my dad phoned to see how "the ladies" were doing. He proceeded to tell us that my husband had bought a golf cart. Our marital limit for spending money without the knowledge of our spouse was set at $50. It was a guess, but I figured the golf cart was much beyond our unwritten spending rule amount. *Oh, was I ever right.* Rick told my dad that the vehicle was worth $1,300, but he got it for only $500 and was planning on making a profit selling it—which is all fine and good, IF you don't have a $50 check-with-your-spouse-LIMIT. I wondered what kind of a piece-a-junk, Lawrence-Welk, 1962 golf cart he found for only $500!

Two days before I was to return home, Rick had to fly to Texas for flight safety recurrent training. I knew his class schedule... and when he wouldn't be able to answer the phone. So I left a message with this fictitious story: "I found this great set of cooking pots on sale for only $500. They are normally $1,300. I was just checking in with you to see if I could get them. The sale ends today and the store is closing in about an hour. If you don't call back, I'm going to get them because I really need them and this is a great deal!" Note the dollar amounts I used. I was amazed that I made it through the message without even a snicker of laughter.

Later that night Rick called. He never suspected a *thing*! Right off I asked, "I know we haven't talked about our spending limit in a long time. It used to be $50, but what is it now?" After a long pause, Rick choked out, "$500," *saving himself!*

"WOW! What's gotten into you? Did you buy something?????" I pried. He confessed to the golf cart purchase. I confessed to fibbing about the pots.

A few months later, Rick was out of town so I took the opportunity to put this ad on Craig's List: "Golf Cart for Sale ... Cheap! Husband bought it while wife was away. Wife selling it while husband is away. Hurry!" That was the weekend I learned that golf carts are legitimate vehicles with pink slips and registration. Shoot. It was a valiant attempt on my part.

Setting an absent-spouse spending limit was one of our first financial decisions together. The first amount in our poor-starving-college-student-days was $15. If we both spent $15 in the same week—well, let's just say it was a ramen noodle week for us. Setting the dollar amount is painless. Sticking to it is paramount!

LeT THe good TiMes ROLL

> *A man going on a journey . . . called his servants and entrusted his property to them. To one he gave five talents of money, to another two talents, and to another one talent, each according to his ability. Then he went on his journey. The man who had received the five talents went at once and put his money to work and gained five more. So also, the one with the two talents gained two more. But the man who had received the one talent went off, dug a hole in the ground and hid his master's money. [To the first two men] the master replied, "Well done, good and faithful servant! You have been faithful with a few things; I will put you in charge of many things. Come and share your master's happiness!" . . . For everyone who has will be given more, and he will have an abundance.*
>
> Matthew 25:14–18, 21, 29a

Toilet paper is a family enigma that is here to stay. I have yet to meet a family that consists of two or more members, where one is *not* the Toilet Paper Police. I mean, really. If you're going to buy cheap, flimsy, poke-my-fingers-through TP, then I need to use at least one-and-a-half good spins at each sitting.

I have fond teenage memories of gathering around the family dinner table and listening to my father's rebuke about toilet paper usage violations. The deep, baritone voice commanded, "If you are a scruncher, you need to become a folder." Thus I embarked on my folding days, which have served me well for twenty-something years.

Since my conversion to Coupon Sense, we have, for the first time in our married lives, purchased *quality* toilet paper. Only being familiar with the cheap goods, this new wad feels like 12-ply. Sweet luxury at my disposal. Unknowingly, I married the TP Police, and he stood true to form after the new flannel-soft privy paper appeared in our powder room. Rick yelled from the bathroom, "I hope you're using less toilet paper now that we have this good brand." I reassured him that I was upholding my folding status.

In the early hours of the morning, necessity called and I made enough movements getting out of bed to ensure Rick's wakeful state. After sitting in the dark for several minutes, I yanked on the paper harder than ever and that baby whirled as fast as my front-loading washing machine on full tilt. Rick remarked, "I bet you had to put your arm way over your head to make it spin that fast." Oh, did we laugh. Undeviating from his economical character he added, "You better be rolling that back on there!"

We all need to be mindful of what we have been given, whether TP, talent or teaching. Being wasteful does not honor God, even if no one else sees. Plenty of talent, placed in each of us by the Lord, is stagnant because it is ignored. We are to be good and faithful servants of all that has been entrusted to us. James 1:22 says, "Do not merely listen to the word, and so deceive yourselves. Do what it says."

Who's the TP Police in your home? If you can't think of anyone else, it's probably *you!*

Big Dreams and a Big God

> *For the word of the LORD is right and true; he is faithful in all he does.... We wait in hope for the LORD; he is our help and our shield. In him our hearts rejoice, for we trust in his holy name. May your unfailing love rest upon us, O LORD, even as we put our hope in you.*
>
> Psalm 33:4, 20–22
>
> *Religion that God our Father accepts as pure and faultless is this: to look after orphans and widows in their distress and to keep oneself from being polluted by the world.*
>
> James 1:27

Before Rick and I were married, we both felt that adoption would be part of our family. We didn't know when or from where, but the dream was birthed before we said "I do." Not to sound all spooky, but I had a dream early in our marriage of a little girl with eyes shaped like Rick's and long black hair. Each time a child was born to us, I held them up and thought, "Nope! The little black-haired girl is still not here!" After the third child we figured out that the Lord had shown me our adopted daughter.

In 2006 God nudged us to start the adoption process. In our minds the financial timing was all wrong, which provided the perfect opportunity for God to reveal how he would provide in his way on his time. Our income could not cover the adoption costs, even in our wildest dreams. We have learned, however, that the Lord doesn't place a dream in your heart without a plan to see it through. So we stepped out on the biggest leap of faith in our entire married life and sent off our application for our little girl from Colombia.

Stepping out in faith is scary for me, because I could not formulate a plan of how God was going to take care of this. Oh, to have God's blueprint of the plan that was in action in my hot little hand! However, that would have eliminated the required faith on my part.

God has placed his heart for orphans in many families, and one such family started a foundation to make adoption grants available. God had this family in mind when He placed the adoption dream in our hearts 24 years ago and used their generosity to cover 10% of our costs. What a blessing to us and to them—allowing them to be a part of bringing another child to their forever family.

Our sister-in-law, Jennie, started a fundraiser by sewing and auctioning homemade purses online. I thought it was brilliant and was moved beyond words to express our appreciation for her time, talent and thoughtfulness. Her first goal was $500, yet in the first year over ten times that much had been raised!

God is so faithful—beyond what we can imagine or think. Has God placed a dream in your heart that is almost forgotten? Dig it up. Dust it off. Step out in faith. He has the means and ways for making your dream a reality.

Mr. Economical

> *Moreover, when God gives any man wealth and possessions, and enables him to enjoy them, to accept his lot and be happy in his work—this is a gift of God. He seldom reflects on the days of his life, because God keeps him occupied with gladness of heart.*
>
> Ecclesiastes 5:19–20

My dear husband prefers the title Mr. Economical over 'Cheapskate' or 'Tightwad.' I like to refer to him as Mr. Wallet. He has earned this thrifty name throughout our 20-plus years of marriage, by continually amazing me at his new and improved *money-saving, penny-pinching schemes* to prosper his family. Albeit these are a few EXTREME examples, they are factual and worth mentioning for posterity.

The Moldy Cantaloupe Conundrum. Somehow a perfectly ripe and inviting cantaloupe snuck its way to the back of the fridge and remained hidden until successfully deformed and fermented. I discovered the disgusting lumpy melon and placed it in the trash. The next morning to my astonishment, the cantaloupe had climbed out of the trash, rolled its lumpy self over to the fridge, pried open the door and scaled the shelves to the most prominent place in the front. OK, Rick found it and put it back in the fridge. Sick! So I put it back in the trash, where it belonged. Later I found it again in the fridge. I conveniently left it there until a friend of mine stopped by and, as she was leaving, I grabbed the rotten fruit and pushed it inside her coat. "Please take this home and throw it away!"

I pleaded. She obliged. And the fridge-garbage-fridge-garbage-fridge cantaloupe was never discussed then . . . or ever again.

The Acrid Trash Bag Affair. Rick's dad visited our house one summer and kindly mowed our gargantuan overgrown lawn. He tediously placed all the clippings in nine garbage bags, ready for transport to the dump. Finding all the trash bags full of grass, Rick carried each one to the back of the property and emptied them down the sloping hill, where he always put the cut grass. Next, being Mr. Economical, he folded the bags now lined with cling-on grass blades and put them at the bottom of our metal, sun-and-heat-absorbing garbage can for future use. Well, 100 degrees + grass clippings in plastic = smelly mess. I believe I did mention the assaulting aroma, but continued to fill the bags until they were used up. Next came a trip to the dump, being there was no garbage removal in our remote town. When we arrived at the crater-size hole half filled with bulging black trash bags, I gasped and exclaimed to my dear husband in an excited voice, "Honey! Look!" He looked, but wasn't quite sure at what. I pointed to the hole and proclaimed, "Look at all the *free* trash bags just waiting to be emptied! We'll never have to buy garbage bags again!" He rolled his eyes toward heaven. I believe he was thanking God for *me*. God was keeping Rick occupied with gladness of heart thanks to me!

canadian coins

> *Drink water from your own cistern, running water from your own well. Should your springs overflow in the streets, your streams of water in the public squares? Let them be yours alone, never to be shared with strangers. May your fountain be blessed, and may you rejoice in the wife of your youth.*
>
> Proverbs 5:15–18

Being a dual citizen of Canada and the USA, you'd think I would be quite familiar with Canadian customs. Truth be told, I never spent more than two weeks per year in my northern homeland until I went to college in British Columbia. My indoctrination in Canadian culture was witnessed by my soon-to-be husband, being that we met on our first day of school. Little did I realize I had plenty to learn. In Canada cars are plugged in to stay warm. (For those of you who are know-it-alls, I was raised in sunny California . . . OK!?) Toppings on pizza are hidden beneath the cheese. Table napkins are called serviettes. One country has Ben-Gay, the other A535, but I can't remember which. Canadians call 18-wheelers "sem-eees" while Americans say "sem-eyes." Canadians go on holidays; Americans go on vacation. The list goes on and on.

One learning experience for me occurred at a checkout stand in a drug store called London Drugs. Rick was chatting with the teller and paying when I found the end of the rainbow. I hit pay dirt, baby. Glancing into the box of matchbooks on the counter, I spied a pile of coins. Someone must have spilled their change purse in the box! Like a bag lady knee-deep in a fountain full of tossed coins, I started grabbing up the money as quickly as my little hands could go. Few and far between are my jackpot moments, so I was exuberantly announcing my own private gold mine while stuffing my pockets.

Rick was beaming from ear to ear, thrilled for my sudden good fortune—or so I thought. As I jingle-jangled my way to the car, Rick couldn't quit laughing. He belly laughed all the way home, just like the little wee-wee-wee piggy. Back at our college he was finally able to spit out, "People pay for matches in Canada!"

"WHAT?!? Why didn't you tell me?!?" I screamed as my criminal behavior became apparent.

"You were so excited. I just couldn't spoil your fun," he lovingly replied.

Every time I read Proverbs 5:18 instructing husbands to rejoice in the wife of their youth, I remember the matchbook coins. Rick was rejoicing in the youth of this wife *and* the wife of his youth. The story still brings a smile to his face when he sees free matches down here in Arizona.

And FYI, next time you're in Canada and need matches, drop some change in the box. You may be contributing to a foreigner's good fortune. (Don't worry, Mom, I sent them a check to pay it all back.)

Frugality at its Finest

> *A wife of noble character who can find? She is worth far more than rubies. Her husband has full confidence in her and lacks nothing of value. She brings him good, not harm, all the days of her life.... She is clothed with strength and dignity; she can laugh at the days to come. She speaks with wisdom, and faithful instruction is on her tongue.*
>
> Proverbs 31:10–12, 25–26

Deep in my heart I feel that Mr. Wallet deserves more than just a single narrative to hail his genius attempts at saving money. (See Mr. Economical from a few pages back.) Early on in our marriage, Lover Boy would buy cards and write lovey-dovey sentiments in them that would cause my eyes to mist and my heart to pitter-patter ... *but* he never wrote my name on the envelopes *nor* licked them shut. Why would anyone waste an envelope on only one recipient? Not like the next gas station greeting card didn't have its own personal wrapper. I asked Rick if he didn't think I was worthy of using up an entire envelope's life. He realized the error of his ways, or so I hoped.

With the knowledge of my envelope-worthiness in mind, Reeko Sauvé continued to buy cards for his loving wife, and he started licking just the teeny-tiny tip of the sticky point—to prove his undying passion for me. Again I inquired if I was not whole-envelope deserving. I hoped that the light went on, but no.

Next, Casanova finally began writing my very own name on the front of the envelope . . . in itty-bitty letters . . . in the top right corner . . . that could eventually be covered by a postage stamp. Where does this kind of thinking come from??? He's too young to remember the Depression-era. *Again,* I explained that my self-worth was plummeting with every postage-stamp-sized depiction bearing my precious given name, the name that should be nearest and dearest to his heart. The light finally went on.

The love letters given to me since that time have *big* bubble letters L-I-N-D-A on the outside, with pictures drawn of birthday cakes and bunnies and Easter eggs, or balloons where the string is a line of loving sentiments swirling around the front of the envelope. Rickey has come full circle, and I have arrived and am now worthy of a complete envelope. It makes my heart glad.

Oftentimes, as wives, we tie our self-worth to our husband's responses to us. The world looks on the outside, but God looks at the heart. We are irresistible to Him, whether we feel like it or not. Our husbands are human, and even if they look like Greek gods to our love-blind eyes, we cannot rest our self-worth on their words alone. We must look to our heavenly God for our true worth.

spreading goodwill

> *Let no corrupt communication proceed out of your mouth, but that which is good to the use of edifying, that it may minister grace unto the hearers. And grieve not the holy Spirit of God, whereby ye are sealed unto the day of redemption. Let all bitterness, and wrath, and anger, and clamor, and evil speaking, be put away from you, with all malice: And be ye kind one to another, tenderhearted, forgiving one another, even as God for Christ's sake hath forgiven you.*
>
> Ephesians 4:29–32, KJV

We are not exactly an eco-friendly home, but we do our small part to save the world by recycling, reducing and reusing. Our main clearing-out happens twice a year—corresponding directly with Rick's bi-annual retraining at FlightSafety in Texas. He is usually gone for four days, and our closets and the garage always have more breathing room when he returns. Rick has a hard time passing garage sales or avoiding the Goodwill, especially when it's 50% off day. I'll admit he has found the rare gem, but in my humble opinion it was just that—rare.

Once when Rick was sitting in the flight simulator in the Lone-Star State, I opened the garage door and the back of the van. I started handing "gems" to the kids to load for Goodwill: a dented Coke sign, a malfunctioning golf putter return, warped plastic storage racks, etc. Relax! Some of it was my junk too. As we drove up to the back of Goodwill to the "Drop Off Zone," one of our boys sternly warned me, "Mom, we cannot go to this

Goodwill. Dad shops at *this one* and he'll buy the same stuff again."

Simply to put your mind at rest, Rick has yet to ask for any "gem" that I hauled away from the house. 'Out of sight, out of mind' is factual.

The entire 3R deal is not only beneficial to our world, but the same 3R's can be useful for keeping our marriages garbage-free. There is an abundance of recycling opportunities in every marriage. Date Night should come through the cycle at least monthly, if not more frequently. Pencil yourself in his calendar, girlfriend! Other pertinent recycling events include praying together, family dinner around the table, Bible reading and gathering with other positive, like-minded couples.

Ephesians 4:29 speaks of reducing the corrupt communication that comes from our mouths. What is corrupt communication you ask? Anything that corrupts. Anything negative. Anything the Holy Spirit tells us not to say, just before we say it anyway.

The flip side of reducing negative talk is reusing good words. Every word we utter should build up and spread grace. Husbands need positive encouragement and the impact of a sweet wife's well-thought-out compliments are the secret weapon to keep her man going. It is the wise woman who reuses her words over and over to build up her husband. Even if a man seems to function effectively on his accomplishments, strengths and talents, his wife's encouragement and her belief in him are paramount to his true success.

Do your part. Recycle, reduce, and reuse.

in sickness and in health

wound-sucking machine

> *Do you not know? Have you not heard? The LORD is the everlasting God, the Creator of the ends of the earth. He will not grow tired or weary, and his understanding no one can fathom. He gives strength to the weary and increases the power of the weak. Even youths grow tired and weary, and young men stumble and fall; but those who hope in the LORD will renew their strength. They will soar on wings like eagles; they will run and not grow weary, they will walk and not be faint.*
>
> Isaiah 40:28–31

The athlete-of-old arose in my husband one Sunday afternoon and he proceeded to join a high school soccer game . . . as the geriatric player. Sadly, he started running too aggressively and separated his Achilles tendon. The short version of the whole story is: four surgeries and three years later, his leg was almost healed. The long version involves gory details of a vacuum wound-sucking machine, crutches, entertaining hallucinations after anesthesia, a knee-high walking boot, a week of confinement on the couch, a wipeout at In-N-Out Burger and a wheelchair scene from New Mexico that I wish we had captured on video.

Rick was a trooper through it all and wanted to get back to work ASAP. He was cleared to fly despite still using crutches and having his wound machine hooked to his belt, with tubes of fluid sticking out of his pant leg. How safe would you feel if your pilot hobbled up to the plane on crutches, wearing a medical device on his hip with liquid-filled hoses leading to his leg? Me either. Rick tried to hide the crutches in the back of the plane, but after the first flight he was assigned a desk job until he was apparatus-free.

Throughout all of the surgeries and recovery times, I honestly tried to be the Titus 2 wife that is loving, reverent, busy at home and kind. But, alas, I failed near the end of Rick's last week of confinement on the couch. One last time, I filled his water glass with ice, added a new bendy straw, made sure his crackers were plentiful and then went to hide in our room upstairs. Not long after I locked the bedroom door, the phone rang and Rick's name appeared on the caller ID. He was calling from his cell phone from the couch downstairs. I unplugged the phone. A break was all I needed—some alone time—maybe a bubble bath with soothing music in the background. Faintly I heard Rick calling my name. I turned on the worship music and began belting out praises to Jesus, drowning out Rick's voice. What could happen to the big guy? He was safe on the couch with the remote, his blankie and his wound-sucking machine.

Praise music is so convicting at times. It's usually times like when you're ignoring your injured husband who is stuck on the sofa. Counting Crows' song kept running though my mind: "If we are the body why aren't His arms reaching? Why aren't His hands healing?" Yeah, yeah, yeah. Not only do sanctified tunes change the atmosphere in your home, they can improve the attitude of your heart as well. Keep the Jesus music on all day long!

Sick Bay—No Way!

> *He who dwells in the shelter of the Most High will rest in the shadow of the Almighty. I will say of the LORD, "He is my refuge and my fortress, my God, in whom I trust." Surely he will save you from the fowler's snare and from the deadly pestilence. He will cover you with his feathers, and under his wings you will find refuge; his faithfulness will be your shield and rampart. You will not fear the terror of night, nor the arrow that flies by day, nor the pestilence that stalks in the darkness, nor the plague that destroys at midday. A thousand may fall at your side, ten thousand at your right hand, but it will not come near you.*
>
> Psalm 91:1–7

Once in a lifetime a vacation opportunity arises that is simply perfect. It was my parent's 50th anniversary, so they decided to treat their three children and spouses to a cruise on the Mexican Riviera. The anticipation leading up to boarding the ship was almost equal to the excitement on the ship and in the ports of call.

Warm sunny skies greeted us every single day on the gorgeous ship as we dined together, played together and relaxed together. Four days into the eight-day trip, however, hand sanitizers began appearing at each door, elevator and bathroom. Day five brought out special employees with spray bottles of sanitizer at the start of each buffet line. That evening the announcements began warning us of the "little guys" that the crew was going to conquer. The captain of the ship, with his thick Norwegian accent, announced that there was indeed a "wirus" that had affected some passengers. He strongly stated that if anyone had signs of the virus, they were to alert the medical staff and stay quarantined in their cabin. What a major bummer to be sick on a cruise!

A couple of times as we passed through the passageways, we came upon cleaning crews that wore outfits that blazingly announced "hazardous materials" across their backs. It reminded me of a scary biochemical contamination movie from my high-school days.

Our family diligently washed our hands and refused to shake hands or touch hand rails. Over and over we claimed Psalm 91:7, "A thousand may fall at your side, ten thousand at your right hand, but it will not come near you." When the numbers were posted online of the final virus count, they totaled more than one-fifth of the passengers on the ship. We counted ourselves as blessed that all eight of us remained healthy, and God protected us from the "plague that destroyed at midday." We believe there is power in the spoken Word of God!

Just as God called everything into existence with the spoken word, our words have power because Christ lives in us. If your marriage is not as you would prefer, follow the advice from Romans 4:17 and call things that are not as though they were: "God has joined us together and no man can separate us. We will overcome evil with good. As for me and my house, we will serve the Lord. My marriage will be honored by all." (See Mark 10:9; Romans 12:21; Joshua 24:15; Hebrews 13:4.)

THe Hairy, THirsTy Man

> *Noah, a man of the soil, proceeded to plant a vineyard. When he drank some of its wine, he became drunk and lay uncovered inside his tent. Ham, the father of Canaan, saw his father's nakedness and told his two brothers outside. But Shem and Japheth took a garment and laid it across their shoulders; then they walked in backward and covered their father's nakedness. Their faces were turned the other way so that they would not see their father's nakedness.*
>
> Genesis 9:20–23

In the hospital recovery room after Rick's third surgery on his leg, I knew something was wrong the minute I laid eyes on him. At home Rick always wears a shirt—always. The only exceptions are when he's showering and swimming. So when I observed my bare-chested husband sitting up and talking loudly and proudly, I realized the anesthesia was still working its wonders.

After giving Rick a lengthy dissertation of the doctor's report, he immediately asked again, "What did the doctor say?" And he kept asking the same question. "Everything is fine," was my pat answer for the next twelve times he inquired. To my shock, Rick started asking for Molson Canadian beer. Loudly. Repeatedly. Rick doesn't drink beer, which I reminded him and tried to convince the skeptical nurse. Lovingly I shushed Rick, "Honey, you've watched the beer commercials from Hockey Night in Canada a few too many times. And you don't drink beer."

"YES, I DO! And they won't bring me my Molson," he bellowed. At that point I informed the nurses that I would not be leaving with the hairy, thirsty man. I planned to wait for my non-alcoholic husband to return. The nurses were cordial and let me wait as long as I needed.

Next, the kleptomaniacs attacked. "Someone stole my wallet and my shoes," Rick whispered in a conspiratorial voice. "No, Honey, they are here under your bed," I confirmed as I displayed the wallet and shoes.

"Someone stole my Molson Canadian!" "No, Rick. You have water and you are embarrassing me. Stop saying you want a beer." Even louder Rick yelled, "I drink beer! But I can't because someone stole my cup!"

Out of nervousness, embarrassment and disbelief, I couldn't stop giggling. My snickers didn't help, obviously, because Rick kept asking in a booming voice, "Why are you laughing? What is so funny?" Oh my. I needed Depends by that point.

When I read in Genesis of Noah being drunk and needing to be covered up, I related to what Shem and Japheth tried to accomplish. A cover-up was necessary! I was not going to be Ham and announce to others the calamity Rick was undergoing. I desired to protect and love my man, covering his delirious wrongdoing. Not only was I in disbelief at the time, but when my real husband mentally returned, he was also in disbelief . . . and nearly needed Depends himself.

Never Underestimate the Value of a Wife!

> *For by the grace given me I say to every one of you: Do not think of yourself more highly than you ought, but rather think of yourself with sober judgment, in accordance with the measure of faith God has given you. Just as each of us has one body with many members, and these members do not all have the same function, so in Christ we who are many form one body, and each member belongs to all the others.*
>
> Romans 12:3–5

Throughout our marriage I have felt appreciated most of the time, but never so much as when the Plague of the Shadow of Death hit. What started as a stomach virus turned into something else that zapped my strength and held me firmly in my bed for five long days of restless sleep. My mother was called in to take care of the children while Rick went to work. It's a blessing that she lives close by and can step into action at a moment's notice.

Every night Rick would return home and relieve my mom of childcare and nursing duty. The concern in his eyes when he looked at me had a depth that I had not witnessed previously. I must have appeared like death warmed over because he was notably worried. He handled the children each evening and then nursed me with tender care.

On the fifth day when I began sitting up in bed and holding food down, relief shone on Rick's good-looking, tanned face. Repeatedly he stated how pleased he was that I was improving.

Then he said the weirdest thing: "Someone is coming over tomorrow to see you." That was all I got out of him—*someone*. Fine. I hoped it was a massage therapist or a maid. Nope, not even close. This is how scared Rick was. It was a nurse practitioner who came to draw my blood for a life-insurance application. Rick realized that the minimal life insurance he had taken out was obviously not going to cover costs if something did take me from him. He was raising my life insurance . . . the first day I was mobile after a week of illness. Surprisingly, my value had risen by thousands of dollars as I lay there moaning. Sitting at the kitchen table with a needle in my arm, I couldn't get over the entire situation. I think the action was supposed to make me feel loved and needed. Not sure if it worked or not? It did amuse me when I likened the incident to Romans 12:3: "Do not think of yourself more highly than you ought."

Is there really a dollar value for what a wife is worth? Sure is. First Corinthians 6:19–20 tells us, "Do you not know that your body is a temple of the Holy Spirit, who is in you, whom you have received from God? You are not your own; you were bought at a price. Therefore honor God with your body." Christ died in our place. Priceless.

selective Hearing

> *Give ear to my words, O LORD, consider my sighing. Listen to my cry for help, my King and my God, for to you I pray. In the morning, O LORD, you hear my voice; in the morning I lay my requests before you and wait in expectation. . . . But let all who take refuge in you be glad; let them ever sing for joy. Spread your protection over them, that those who love your name may rejoice in you. For surely, O LORD, you bless the righteous; you surround them with your favor as with a shield.*
>
> Psalm 5:1–3, 11–12

It's not often that I am at the mercy of a writing pad to communicate with my family. Alas, I awoke one Wednesday morning without a voice. Being a Wednesday, the coupon club I belong to put all the store deals on the net and *oh my!* there were so many freebies and great produce prices. Conveniently, Sprouts, a produce/gourmet grocer, is on my husband's route home from work. I phoned to ask him to pick up some bargains, but I didn't get far with the missing voice and all. He couldn't even understand my whispered "Sprouts." So I found my nine-year-old and wrote "Sprouts" on a little note pad, then handed him the phone. He took the receiver and read "Sprouts" three times at increasing decibels to his father, who I believe needs a hearing test. Rick is a pilot; his hearing is checked every year and he claims that it is fine. The Sprouts phone call proved otherwise (again).

Another hearing-aid-needed incident occurred the following week. My hair isn't long, to say the least, but all the coloring, highlights, hair glue, mousse and hairspray leave it a bit tangled at times. I was combing my wet locks and I mumbled to my husband (the hearing-challenged husband who has yearly hearing exams) that I could use some No More Tangles. "What?" he asked, like I was speaking Swahili again. "No More Tangles." A look of confusion registered on his handsome, yet dumbstruck face. "What?" Enunciating more clearly than the judges from the Scripps Spelling Bee, I uttered *loudly,* "NO MORE TANGLES!" "Oh, I thought you said No More Tangos."

I laughed. That would be a *great* product to market. Anytime someone who thinks they can dance breaks out in a tango, you could just spray them and relieve yourself of the misery. Then I started imagining all the great sprays that would be outstanding performers for the public at large, like "No More Rude People," or my personal favorite, "No More Selective-Hearing Husbands."

How often do we look to the Lord and ask as David did in the Psalms, "Give ear to my words, O LORD"? God hears our prayers, but sometimes we feel the need to prompt Him to listen to us. Should the tables be turned? Does God need to ask us to hear what He is saying? Are we using selective hearing if we only listen to God when it suits our fancy? Maybe I should market the spray, "No More One-Way Prayers."

Hats Off to Florence and Clara

> *"'I was hungry and you gave me something to eat, I was thirsty and you gave me something to drink, I was a stranger and you invited me in, I needed clothes and you clothed me, I was sick and you looked after me, I was in prison and you came to visit me.' Then the righteous will answer him, 'Lord, when did we see you hungry and feed you, or thirsty and give you something to drink? When did we see you a stranger and invite you in, or needing clothes and clothe you? When did we see you sick or in prison and go to visit you?' The King will reply, 'I tell you the truth, whatever you did for one of the least of these brothers of mine, you did for me.'"*
>
> Matthew 25:35–40

There are plenty of unusual yet factual experiences I could include on a resume such as travel guide in London, steel worker, or runway model. (I was five years old, okay?) Yet in all my years of teaching and being a hockey mom/wife, there are no medical related experiences to account for. When God knit me together, He did not include a strong stomach or a passion to aid the wounded. Even after glancing through an emergency medical guide, I had nightmares for days.

Unfortunately, for both Rick and me, he separated his Achilles tendon, and throughout four surgeries my nursing skills—or lack thereof—were called upon. The initial evening at home after surgery #1, I knew we were in trouble. My instructions were to remove the bandage, rinse the incision, apply ointment and rewrap. Sounded simple enough. Following my first view of my sweet husband's post-op leg, I gagged and heaved in our bedroom closet for several minutes. Honestly, I tried to rinse the wound, but accompanying my weak stomach is the automatic closing of my eyes. Rick was lying face down on the bed, probably wondering what was taking so long. He finally told me to leave and he conducted his own post-op care.

Surgery #3 brought home a gaping leg hole, a wound-sucking machine and, thank the good Lord, a visiting at-home nurse. (Not me!) I thought I was getting off scot-free until she instructed me to watch the informational video on the wound-sucking machine. Previously I had viewed an instructional video for our washing machine. How different could it be? Three minutes was all I could stand, so I shut it off. What good is it to have a video playing while my eyes are closed and my involuntary choking noises drowned out the video lady? The nurse actually planned to train me on the wound-sucking machine herself. Oh, she couldn't have chosen a more incompetent assistant. I flat out refused.

That whole sickness and health part of our marriage vows has been conveniently divided for our marriage. Rick does sickness. I do health. Plain and simple. Thankfully for Rick, "a man's spirit sustains him in sickness" (Proverbs 18:14) and "by [Jesus'] wounds we are healed" (Isaiah 53:5), because I was of no help sustaining or healing him at all.

All I can say is Florence Nightingale and Clara Barton are my heroines forever!

The Invisible Invalid

> *You must obey my laws and be careful to follow my decrees. I am the LORD your God. Keep my decrees and laws, for the man who obeys them will live by them. I am the LORD. Keep my commands and follow them. I am the LORD. Follow my decrees and be careful to obey my laws, and you will live safely in the land.*
>
> Leviticus 18:4–5; 22:31; 25:18

The day before our family headed to San Diego, Rick mentioned that he had not been feeling well for a while, should probably have seen the doctor, but was looking forward to relaxing on the beach. We had a blast the first day going whale watching, touring a lighthouse and peering inside tide pools, but all that excitement was a bit too much for Superman.

Rick's dangly dealie at the back of his throat, which we later learned is called a uvula, was swollen and causing him major discomfort. When I awoke the following morning, Rick was sitting on the edge of the bed with a stressed look on his face. Barely opening his mouth, he explained that he could hardly breathe and he had called for an ambulance. To top it off and bring a measure of assurance to his wife, he added, "This is as close to dying as I've ever felt." I remained calm, prayed furiously, got everyone up and dressed and prepared to follow the ambulance to the hospital.

The ER got Rick checked in promptly. With three hungry children, I waited for comforting news about Rick's diagnosis and then drove off to find food. Fortunately, there were restaurants near the hospital. Unfortunately, I didn't pay attention when following the ambulance and could not find the way back to our hotel. After an hour we eventually located it, but weren't in the room ten minutes before Rick phoned for us to come and retrieve his now heavily medicated self. Seems he had an infection and required some antibiotics.

When the children and I returned to the ER, the nurse informed us that he had been discharged and was probably at the pharmacy across the street filling a prescription. We checked throughout the pharmacy and couldn't locate our husband/father. After the pharmacist denied seeing a 5'8" man with black hair and a blue shirt, I instructed the children to search for their father in the bushes all the way back to the hospital. This proved fruitless. I was aware that someday Rick would disappear in the twinkling of an eye, but I was planning on traveling with him. Our third trip into the ER was a success. Rick *was* there, and the confused nurse was nowhere to be seen.

God had to include so many specific verses in the Bible to guide men in their daily tasks and responsibilities. One such verse is Matthew 9:12: Jesus said, "It is not the healthy who need a doctor, but the sick." Obviously there was going to be an issue with men avoiding the doctor, so God made it plain and simple ahead of time in His Word. But do men follow this clear instruction? No! At least not the man at my house. It only took one night of clogged breathing to help Rick believe that the sick need a doctor . . . just like Jesus said.

HOW TO EAT FRESH WORMS

> *Meanwhile his disciples urged him, "Rabbi, eat something." But he said to them, "I have food to eat that you know nothing about." Then his disciples said to each other, "Could someone have brought him food?" "My food," said Jesus, "is to do the will of him who sent me and to finish his work."*
>
> John 4:31–34

It was late summer and I was caring for the vegetable garden of a friend who was on holidays. (Canadians go on holidays. Americans go on vacation.) We were living in High Level, Alberta, a booming northern town of 2,000 inhabitants where the sun never slid behind the horizon in summer. So much sunshine produced mammoth vegetables worthy of ribbons at a county fair. My friend instructed me to harvest, freeze and eat as much as my husband and I could manage while they were gone. Every day I hauled bags of fresh peas, broccoli, beans, leafy lettuce and corn to our home. I was in salad bar heaven.

Rick was flying for a small aviation company where, with so much daylight, they could fly almost 20 hours a day. Daily I packed a lunch and dinner for my husband because there were no places to eat on the remote strips where he was landing. Being blessed with fresh veggies, I loaded him up with meals that would make Peter Rabbit's heart palpitate.

One morning Rick left the house around 7:00 a.m. and I began blanching and freezing the vegetables. I was three hours into my task when I plopped two heads of chopped broccoli crowns into boiling water. This same broccoli was earlier loaded into a Ziploc baggie in Rick's lunch. As soon as the hot water penetrated the broccoli flowers, worms floated to the surface. Lime green wriggling worms—12 to 15 living but dying-very-quickly worms. Eeewww. It reminded me of the time Jesus told His disciples that he had food they knew nothing about. Me too.

Immediately I dialed the number for the airport, hoping to catch Rick between flights to warn him of the hidden protein in his sack lunch. Surprisingly, Rick answered the phone. Not wanting to cause alarm, I asked how he was doing. Fine. Then I pried, "Did you eat your lunch yet?" hoping I had intercepted the ingestion of grubs since it was only 10:00 a.m. Unfortunately, Rick replied, "Yes, I did. I just finished. It was great. Thanks." "Good. See you tonight. Bye." And I swiftly hung up before he could ask any questions.

A prayer was sent heavenward for my husband's stomach of steel to ward off any ill effects. I remembered John the Baptist eating locusts (see Mark 1:6) and asked God to keep Rick alive just as He had John. God answered my prayers, and my worm-filled husband returned home safely. Late that night under the cover of darkness in our bedroom, I confessed to feeding worms to Rick. We laughed and laughed while tears flooded our eyes. Despite his wormy breath, I even kissed him good night.

THE BEST MEDICINE

> *A happy heart makes the face cheerful, but heartache crushes the spirit. . . . All the days of the oppressed are wretched, but the cheerful heart has a continual feast. . . . A cheerful look brings joy to the heart, and good news gives health to the bones. . . . A cheerful heart is good medicine, but a crushed spirit dries up the bones.*
>
> Proverbs 15:13, 15, 30; 17:22

I am convinced that God created laughter as a coping mechanism for marriage. What better way to ruin a good argument than to make the other person laugh? In our early years of marriage, there was a song by Weird Al Yankovich entitled Yoda, sung to the tune of Lola by the Kinks. Yes, I'm dating myself. No matter how mad we were, if one of us started singing "Yoda, yo yo yo, Yoda," we were able to crack through the tension and ended up smiling and finally chuckling together. It worked every time, even in the midst of tears and hurt feelings.

We took a marriage course which recommended that after an argument, the offending person should apologize and then add, "Let's go on from here." Being just a bit off-kilter ourselves, Rick and I found this to be hilarious. From that moment on, after every "I'm sorry" the line, "Let's go on from here," was repeated in a lusty, mimicking, soap-opera voice.

Besides having the Lord at the center of our relationship, laughing together has been high on the list of "glue" that has held us together. Rick is a prankster at heart. Likewise, I'm sure he would say that I am too. The difference is that I don't lie awake at night dreaming up acts of tomfoolery. I'm convinced he does.

On April Fool's Day we proceed with caution in the Crosby house. You never know what could be awaiting you to be scared, soaked, zapped, etc. Late one March 31st, Rick snuck out of our bedroom and put a rubber band around the spray nozzle at the kitchen sink and then aimed it straight out. To the amusement of the entire family, the following morning Rick forgot about his sabotage and blasted himself. I appeared in the kitchen ten seconds after the blast and asked, "Why is your shirt all wet?" The kids and Rick all howled like crazed hyenas, but didn't answer my question. Of course, I was the next rubber-banded-nozzle victim.

Medical evidence shows that laughter is healing and life-giving. God created us to laugh in order to relieve stress, to reduce tension and to rejoice with each other. Revisit some moments of hilarity in your own marriage. Have a 'remember when . . .' night with your spouse and bring healing to your bones.

Pre-Book-Signing Nightmare

> *Pharaoh said to Joseph, "I had a dream, and no one can interpret it. But I have heard it said of you that when you hear a dream you can interpret it." "I cannot do it," Joseph replied to Pharaoh, "but God will give Pharaoh the answer he desires."*
>
> Genesis 41:15–16

I'm normally a fairly level-headed woman who deals with new situations and opportunities with glee. I thought I was ably handling the pressure of my first book signing for *Laughter in the Midst of Mothering*. However, I realized when I awoke from a nightmare that I must have been suppressing inner turmoil about the event. The dream was entertaining, nonetheless.

I dreamt that the alarm was not set, so I overslept. The air got sucked out of my lungs as I realized my dilemma. The book signing started at 11:00 a.m.; in my dream I awoke at 12:15 confused and flustered. It was *so real!* I couldn't figure out if it was 3:00 or 12:15 . . . you know, because the clock hands could be reversed. Funny how your mind plays trick on you even in your sleep. Then my father called me from the bookstore to ask where I was, and to tell me that the highway north of us was flooded and I would need to go the long way around. I began sobbing and mumbling.

I went to find my husband, whose fault it was for not setting the alarm. Rick was watching a movie in a theater room that we don't have. I told him over and over that we were late and he was to blame. His brown eyes were glued to the big screen. He didn't seem too interested in my plight. So I went over and beat on him with the back of my wrists—you know, like an orangutan. (Dreams are great, aren't they??) Next, I went upstairs, did my hair and threw on my clothes, crying all the while. Back downstairs I told Rick that he had to drive so I could apply my makeup in the car. He had moved to the workout room (that we don't have) and was busy clanging weights, not even looking at me or acknowledging me. Another primate beating occurred.

Then I woke up. It was over. I hadn't actually acted like a monkey. The alarm was set. My husband was asleep next to me. He didn't buy a theater room or gym without checking with me first. And there was time to make it to the book signing. Whew.

Dreams can mess with your mental health, can't they? So often dreams have interpretations that are applicable to our lives, if we take the time to ask God what He is trying to teach us. I have formulated my own meaning of the orangutan beating: even when I'm asleep I blame Rick for my mistakes and shortcomings. It brought to my awareness the need for taking responsibility for my own actions. It's so easy to blame your spouse, but it doesn't make for a merry marriage. Own up, sister. I'm right there with you.

God said that young men will see visions and old men will dream dreams (see Acts 2:17). He omitted the part about 40-something women having orangutan nightmares.

SCHEDULING CONFLICTS

> "Do not judge, or you too will be judged. For in the same way you judge others, you will be judged, and with the measure you use, it will be measured to you. Why do you look at the speck of sawdust in your brother's eye and pay no attention to the plank in your own eye? How can you say to your brother, 'Let me take the speck out of your eye,' when all the time there is a plank in your own eye? You hypocrite, first take the plank out of your own eye, and then you will see clearly to remove the speck from your brother's eye."
>
> Matthew 7:1–5

With every year that comes my way I find new and exciting occupations that I had no idea existed. One year I learned about proctologists. Visiting this doc was not jovial or pleasant. I won't go into details, but I discovered that I was in need of a minor surgery and could schedule it at my convenience, as long as it was on a Thursday. I was in moderate pain and desired to take care of the situation ASAP.

Late that night, I asked my husband when would be best for him to take off a Thursday and Friday from his flying schedule. He glanced over his calendar and fired off, "Not February 23rd, March 1st, or the 8th. The 15th won't work either, or the 22nd. The 29th I'm out of town. How about the 5th of April?"

Normally, I'm a levelheaded woman who can discuss scheduling conflicts like I'm ordering pizza. Add a little bit of pain to my already tapped-out life and I could fall apart without a moment's notice. Putting off my take-me-out-of-pain surgery for seven weeks sent me over the top. I couldn't believe my sweet husband was being so inconsiderate. I came a bit unglued. I spat. I sputtered. Tears clouded my eyes and I yelled, "I'm sorry I'm such a huge inconvenience in your life that you can't take time out of your schedule for me!" In retrospect, those were not words that made me proud.

Without waiting for a reply, I went into the bathroom and climbed in the shower. It is the only place in the house where I can cry alone. While standing under the warm water feeling sorry for myself, I heard the Lord speak in that still, small voice, "That's how I feel." Just great. While I was sulking and mad at my husband, the Lord was using my own words to remind me that I had been neglecting Him. I had been treating my time with the Lord as a huge inconvenience in my life. He's so like that—to use the splinter in my husband's eye to point out the log in mine.

Repentance brings such a freeing feeling, I should remember to do it more often. The Lord is daily waiting for us. It's up to us to fit Him into our schedules.

P.S. Thankfully, my surgery was scheduled that same week.

DO YOU REALLY WANT TO HURT ME?

> *Do not let any unwholesome talk come out of your mouths, but only what is helpful for building others up according to their needs, that it may benefit those who listen. Be kind and compassionate to one another, forgiving each other, just as in Christ God forgave you.*
>
> Ephesians 4:29, 32

October 31st, 2005 went down in the Crosby family history books as the hallowed eve when I poisoned my husband.

Rick and I escorted our three children, along with our two overnight visitors, to our church's October Fest. By 9:30 p.m. my peaceful home was calling to me. As we herded our flock toward the van, my husband announced his plans to go to a late show since he had movie passes that expired that night. I wasn't impressed, to say the least. To his credit, Rick did help deposit all five kids in the van—the same children who had been consuming gross amounts of sugar for the past three hours.

"All candy on the kitchen counter. Costumes off. Jammies on. Teeth brushed for five minutes." With four kids finally in bed, I set Bibleman on our bathroom counter to look at a bloody toe. Two weeks previously, he had slammed his big toe and the nail had come off. The pediatrician had given me instructions to rinse it with a solution of 50/50 hydrogen peroxide and water. Conveniently, there sat a clear plastic bottle with only three ounces of water, so I doubled it with hydrogen peroxide. The toe was washed, medicated, bandaged and, as soon as Bibleman was tucked in, I fell into bed exhausted.

At 2:09 a.m. I was shaken awake by my husband's hands and his booming, panicky voice hollering, "Linda, what was in my water bottle next to the sink?" Oh no!

"Hydrogen peroxide," I groggily answered.

He grabbed the peroxide bottle and loudly read, "If ingested, call the Poison Control Center immediately. Where is the number for Poison Control?"

I am not super sympathetic when I am fully awake. I am on the verge of completely unconcerned when I am half asleep. My eyes still closed, I offered, "In the phone book under P," and drifted off back to sleep.

When I awoke the next morning, I glanced over to see my husband's back and the entire hydrogen peroxide nightmare resurfaced. His breathing was undetectable. Was Rick dead? I gave him a little shove. Praise be to God, he groaned.

Guilt tried to consume me, but a twinge of "serves him right" was just under the surface, due to being sent home with five candy-laden children. I came so close to making it through my apology without grinning, "I'm sorry I almost poisoned you."

James 3:8 speaks of the tongue being full of deadly poison. Nothing will destroy a marriage quicker than the poison of an uncontrolled tongue. Daily (even hourly sometimes!) we need to heed the truth in Ephesians (see above) and in Proverbs 18:21: "The tongue has the power of life and death, and those who love it will eat its fruit." Keep your marriage poison free!

THE MiDNiGHT PHONE CALL

> *Now the body is not made up of one part but of many. . . But in fact God has arranged the parts in the body, every one of them, just as he wanted them to be. If they were all one part, where would the body be? As it is, there are many parts, but one body. The eye cannot say to the hand, "I don't need you!" And the head cannot say to the feet, "I don't need you!" On the contrary, those parts of the body that seem to be weaker are indispensable, and the parts that we think are less honorable we treat with special honor.*
>
> 1 Corinthians 12:14, 18–23a

My sweet husband reluctantly sent me away on a three-day scrapbooking retreat. It was a much-needed rest from home responsibilities, and I didn't care if I accomplished much scrapbooking or not. As a father of three children, this was Rick's first time being left alone with all three children—the cooking . . . the diapers . . . a trip to church. I couldn't wait to hear how he managed without wifey-poo.

Just past midnight on my first night away, my bunk-bed blankets were just warming up when the pay phone in the hall rang. Some ardent scrapper answered the phone, stuck her head in our room and queried, "Is Linda still awake?"

My husband's words did not bring comfort to my soul. He had been alone with the children for less than 12 hours and our six-year-old had put her arm through a window trying to "scare a cat out of our yard." All the fish died due to a foreign substance being added to the fish tank. Bologna sandwich? Play-doh? Who knew? But the reason for his call? He was on his way to the hospital with our three-year-old son who smacked the back of his head on the bathtub. Was he bathing the child at midnight? I didn't ask.

After the details dribbled through the phone lines, I think Rick expected me to say I was rushing home to save him. My words did not bring comfort to my husband's soul. Unless someone died, I wasn't going home. Truthfully, what could I do to help anyway? Guard the unbroken windows? I did call the following morning to check the status on the home front. All was well, and I resumed scrapbooking with much relief.

There were several more phone calls over the weekend: How do you get the rabbit back in the cage? Is there any more toilet paper somewhere? Are the dishes in the dishwasher clean or dirty? It was news to me that I held so much family information in strictest confidence.

Looking back at the weekend of the midnight phone call, I'm thankful that my hubby allowed me to leave for some R&R. However, I'm more grateful that men can survive with all the wifely duties under their command. It makes them appreciate the juggling act wives perform daily, and it gives them deep insight into the myriad of responsibilities they have bestowed upon us—the weaker vessel—and just how worthy we are of a weekend escape.

TO LOVE AND TO CHERISH

TURBAN OR FEATHER?

> *The LORD is compassionate and gracious, slow to anger, abounding in love. He will not always accuse, nor will he harbor his anger forever; he does not treat us as our sins deserve or repay us according to our iniquities. For as high as the heavens are above the earth, so great is his love for those who fear him; as far as the east is from the west, so far has he removed our transgressions from us.*
>
> Psalm 103:8–12

When I initially called home from college and told my parents that I had met this amazing guy, my dad and mom were all ears. Amorously, I detailed Rick's charming personality, as well as his black hair, brown eyes, dark skin . . . which brought the question from my mother, "What nationality is he?" "Indian," I replied. My dad's next inquiry went down in the family history books as one of the best questions of all time. "Turban or feather?" Not that it would have mattered to them, as long as Rick loved me and loved the Lord. "Feather. He's Cree from Quebec," I explained. My family has loved Rick from the moment they met him. My brother and sister went as far as accusing him of being mom's new favorite child.

Following along the same theme, when Rick took out my dad for "the talk" to ask for my hand in marriage, he discussed everything he could think of *except me* for over 90 minutes. Finally he relented and said to my father, "Well, I guess you know why I asked you here tonight." Another great dad reply emerged, "Yes, but I'm not going to make this easy on you." Hahahahahhahhahhaaaaahhhhha (snort) hahahahha! Oh, to have been a fly on the greasy wall at that restaurant! Finally Rick brought up the *real* topic, "I was wondering if Linda could visit my teepee?" It was my dad's turn to laugh.

My dad's advice to Rick that day was, "Just love her." After 22 years, I must say Rick has done just that, no matter what. Through thick and thin (literally), through laughing and crying, through joy and heartache—even when I backed the car over his hockey equipment—he still loved me.

As a wife my aim is to serve my husband by "just loving him" as well. Irritations and uncomfortable situations are inevitable, but how I choose to react to them shows exactly how much love I'm serving up. I'm not able to control what comes my way, but with God's help I am fully able to control how I deal with each circumstance. I'm thankful the Lord is abounding in grace and forgiveness, and removes my sins as far as the east is from the west. I need to dish up more of that grace on a juicy platter for my husband.

In Proverbs Solomon had much to share about dealing with struggles between people: "love covers over all wrongs" (10:12b); "he who covers over an offense promotes love" (17:9a); and "starting a quarrel is like breaching a dam; so drop the matter before a dispute breaks out" (17:14). "Just love her" covers all of these as well. My dad is so smart.

Dairy Queen Departures

> *Our mouths are filled with laughter, our tongues with songs of joy. Then it was said among the nations, "The LORD has done great things for them." The LORD has done great things for us, and we are filled with joy.*
>
> Psalm 126:2–3

Most families would jump at the opportunity to visit the local Dairy Queen for Peanut Buster Parfaits, Dilly Bars and Blizzards. Not the Crosby family. We have been scarred for life at the hands of our husband/father and his idea of a 'good time.' "Anyone want to go to Dairy Queen?" is unhappily answered by, "Nope!" "Not me!" "No thanks, Dad!" and "NO WAY!" The children look at me with large eyes pleading, "Please, don't make us go with *him!*" One would think we are torturing our children in the ice-cream establishment. Not so.

The exact origin of the tradition is a mystery, but it is alive and well in the Crosby household. Nothing out of the ordinary occurs during ordering or eating. It's the leaving that is so special. Rick will not depart without saying goodbye to everyone in the restaurant, customers and employees alike, purposely wearing some of his ice cream on his face. The reactions he receives are actually quite entertaining, but the children always miss this part because they make a bee-line for the nearest exit, closely followed by their mother.

Secretly we know the kids think Rick's dorky tradition is pretty funny, but they will never admit it. The real reason Rick upholds the sticky face routine is to make everyone laugh:

the employees, the customers, the Crosbys and anyone brave enough to go with us to DQ.

Proverbs tells us, "A merry heart maketh a cheerful countenance" (15:13, KJV) and "A merry heart doeth good like a medicine" (17:22, KJV). God designed laughter with many positive physical effects: lowered blood pressure, reduced stress hormones, increased muscle flexion and boosted immune functions. Laughter also triggers the release of endorphins, the body's natural painkillers.

Have you noticed the more stress in your life, the less you laugh? How much stress are you carrying around? Have you laughed today? The Lord is waiting for you to use His natural painkiller and have a hearty laugh. He's also available to carry that stress load for you.

Set the laughing example in your home today . . . or visit Dairy Queen and start a new family tradition. You may think an ice-cream-covered face is stupid or ridiculous, but I triple-dog-dare you to try to say goodbye to everyone at DQ without laughing and/or eliciting laughs. It can't be done.

THE BLUE FLOWER BOOK

> *Love is patient, love is kind. It does not envy, it does not boast, it is not proud. It is not rude, it is not self-seeking, it is not easily angered, it keeps no record of wrongs. Love does not delight in evil but rejoices with the truth. It always protects, always trusts, always hopes, always perseveres. Love never fails.*
>
> 1 Corinthians 13:4–8a

Three months after our marriage ceremony I happened on a radio broadcast of Focus on the Family where Dr. Dobson had a guest marriage counselor on the show. He told a depressing story about a couple who had been married over 50 years. He asked the couple what the problem was in their marriage, and the woman pulled a book from her purse, plopped it on the counselor's desk and announced, "Here is a record of everything my husband has done wrong for the past 50 years." Mercy sakes alive! At the end of the radio show, the counselor made a comment that struck my heart, "Just think where that couple would be if she had kept track of the nice things her husband had done for 50 years!"

That very day I went out and purchased a blue cloth-bound journal with pressed flowers on the cover. I figured the floral arrangement would deter Rick from opening the book if I ever left it out. It became my stealth mission of love as I recorded the nice things he had done for me, how much I admired him and the funny times we experienced together.

Reading back through the Blue Flower Book now, I realize how enamored I was with Rick's thick, wavy black hair. His locks are referenced more than 20 times, I'm sure. Maybe I was subliminally hoping his hair would stay forever . . . and most of it has. Only slight relocation has occurred.

Being enraptured as newlyweds, I assumed the 140-page journal would be filled in mere months. However, life got in the way a few times . . . and our "newlyweddedness" faded as well. It took three and a half years for me to complete the volume of love.

Christmas Eve 1990 was the chosen date for the presentation of the Blue Flower Book. Tears gathered in my eyes as Rick opened "the last" Christmas gift. Consequently, it became a moment worthy of some sappy TV sitcom when Rick looked at the flowers, looked at me, looked back at the flowers. Finally he flipped through the pages and half asked, half stated, "You wrote this whole book? Wow! I'll read it later," and he set is aside. Through much persuasion and recognition of the error on his part as to how thrilled he should have been, he did indeed read the entire journal that night. Oh, did we howl with laughter as we relived happy times.

Today the Blue Flower Book stays in Rick's bedside table. On days when I have obviously forgotten how wonderful he is, Rick pulls it out and reads aloud about pastimes when I thought he was a fabulous husband. It works every time. Love keeps no record of wrongs.

ROADWAY GLAMOUR SHOTS

> *You, therefore, have no excuse, you who pass judgment on someone else, for at whatever point you judge the other, you are condemning yourself, because you who pass judgment do the same things. . . . For it is not those who hear the law who are righteous in God's sight, but it is those who obey the law who will be declared righteous.*
>
> Romans 2:1, 13

Confession time again. I received a speeding ticket for driving 48 mph in a 25 zone—in my dad's 1966 shiny, red Mustang. It's hard *not* to speed in that car, but at least the officer was cordial. I did the crime and I paid my time in traffic school. The instructor surprised me with the content of the class, where close to 25% of my valuable time was spent hearing about how photo radar tickets are usually bunk. He described how they are illegally taken from private property, how a signature is required to profess guilt and how the photos usually aren't clear enough to prove the identity of the driver. Being a lover of safety rules, I had a hard time with this, as you can imagine—not the photo radar, but the instructor freely sharing the information on the city's dime. No doubt the city had no idea what their instructor was instructing.

It was late when I arrived home after my graduation from my second night in traffic school, and Rick, my dear husband, was giving me a hard time about breaking the law. This was a bit surprising to me as his traffic violations outnumbered mine four to one. He was opening the mail as he harassed me... and he suddenly grew silent. He was staring at a letter, so I glanced over to see a *photo radar ticket* with HIS name on it. OK, I laughed out loud at my husband. Not a very supportive wife, I know. I firmly believe Numbers 32:23 which says, "You may be sure that your sin will find you out." Being a wise woman, I did keep that verse to myself right then, despite my laughter.

To make a hilarious story short, we drove down to the courthouse to view the picture (this was back in the day before they mailed them). The kind man handed us the picture. At that exact moment Rick was wearing the very same navy and yellow striped shirt that he sported for the roadway glamour shot. In the picture he was also wearing his Top Gun Aviator Ray Ban sunglasses, which were hanging from the front of his same navy and yellow striped shirt. I barely held in a giggle. "I don't think it looks like you," I reassured my lawbreaking husband.

He did the crime and paid his time. What are the chances of showing up in the same clothes weeks later??? It was a moment worthy of Candid Camera.

Wanted: Moving Boxes

> *The LORD God formed the man from the dust of the ground and breathed into his nostrils the breath of life, and man became a living being. . . . But for Adam no suitable helper was found. So the LORD God caused the man to fall into a deep sleep; and while he was sleeping, he took one of the man's ribs and closed up the place with flesh. Then the LORD God made a woman from the rib he had taken out of the man, and he brought her to the man.*
>
> Genesis 2:7, 20b–22

Recently I saw a video where a man was describing the difference between the brains of men and women. It was choice! He described a woman's brain as a conglomeration of interconnecting wires that have multiple pieces of information flying from here to there at all times. Every thought is mysteriously connected to every other thought. I believe this is true. Even in my sleep I can't turn off the thoughts and ideas. I wake up at 3:27 a.m. and mentally add items to my grocery list, rearrange furniture and plot out the garden.

Next, the brilliant gentleman explained how a man's brain functions, and I found it to be shockingly true as well. He said there are thousands of little boxes in every man's head. Each box holds specific information for a single event or idea. None of the boxes ever touch each other. EVER. The peculiar thing is that *only one box* can be opened at a time. If a conversation shifts gears, he must close the first box in order to open the next box that applies. *And*, most importantly, the box that men usually have open is *the empty box*. This explains a lot, doesn't it, girls?

I used to think my dear husband was hearing impaired when I had to repeat things to him. Now I realize that he was busy closing the empty box, so that he could open the box I was talking about. No wonder he gets tired of having in-depth conversations with me! Think of all the work involved.

I let my daughter watch the video so that she would have a greater understanding of the opposite sex. I wish I had known this truth when I was her age. She laughed, and I thought that was the last of her response. Au contraire. One Sunday we were driving to church and I asked Rick a question about our afternoon hockey activities. No response. After a few seconds, I heard a voice quietly drift from the back seat, *"Close the empty box. Open the hockey box."* Of course Rick didn't hear that because he was in mental motion. Then he said, "What?" And the females burst out with peals of laughter, bringing on another more forceful, *"What?"*

Personally, I think the missing rib was the one that connected the boxes, and . . . well, it was permanently removed thousands of years ago by the God who created the empty box.

great expectations

> *A man reaps what he sows. The one who sows to please his sinful nature, from that nature will reap destruction; the one who sows to please the Spirit, from the Spirit will reap eternal life. Let us not become weary in doing good, but at the proper time we will reap a harvest if we do not give up. Therefore, as we have opportunity, let us do good to all people, especially to those who belong to the family of believers.*
>
> Galations 6:7b–10

ex-pec-ta-tion [ek-spek-tey-sh*uh* n] noun

1. the act or the state of expecting
2. the act or state of looking forward or anticipating
3. something expected
4. a prospect of future good

After being married for about fifteen minutes, both Rick and I figured out that we had some post-marital expectations. He expected that we would be buying crunchy peanut butter, but I'm a Skippy smooth girl to the core. I expected Rick to pop out of bed on Sunday mornings and make yummy breakfasts of scrambled eggs, bacon and pancakes shaped in my initials—just like my daddy did—but Rick sleeps in as long as possible on Sundays. Rick expected his wife to go to every single hockey game like his mommy did, but I have other things to do sometimes. I expected hotel vacations, but Rick brought a tent and two sleeping bags into this marriage. Rick expected to have his socks folded into long tubes, but I made sock balls . . . until I was retrained.

Expectations. We all have 'em. In marriage they can lead to disappointment, can't they? Sometimes, however, our true disappointments are rooted in unrealistic expectations. We expect our husbands to treat us like their queens, and to know telepathically what birthday gift we would adore. Truth be told, we don't exactly act like royalty, and most married men need birthday-gift buying assistance. We have to be honest with each other and with ourselves about what we are expecting. If I expect Rick home each night for dinner at 6:00, but he can't always arrive by then, I need to relax and focus on the nights he does scoot in the chair at the head of the table 'on time.' I need to let go of the 'every night' expectation and go with what is reasonable. It makes no sense for me to be angry with him when the situation is out of his hands regarding traffic, meetings, flights, etc.

If it will help clear the expectational air in your marriage, both of you should make a list of your top five expectations from your spouse. Share the lists together and talk about which ones are reasonable and which ones simply aren't attainable. Having this discussion will free both of you from walking on egg shells and playing the guessing game. Reading your spouse's list also gives you at least a target for keeping your man happy. When we know what is expected of us, we will not grow weary in well doing.

CaLL Me LiTTLe ReD

> *Encourage one another and build each other up, just as in fact you are doing. Now we ask you, [sisters], to respect those who work hard among you, who are over you in the Lord and who admonish you. Hold them in the highest regard in love because of their work. Live in peace with each other.*
>
> 1 Thessalonians 5:11–13

When we were living in Fort Vermilion, Alberta, a decision was made to venture down to the city. . . . a nine-hour drive to fast food. An average temperature for January was -35°C, causing the logging dirt road to be frozen and saving us three hours of driving time by taking the back road straight to Edmonton. The Northern lights surprisingly lit the night sky as well as the seven-foot snow banks on each side of the "highway." It was like driving in an Olympic luge tube, minus the bobsled.

A few hours from home, I mentioned to Rick from beneath my fur-lined parka hood that I saw something on the road ahead. As he slowed down we came upon a wolf pack running down the highway. There were six or seven full grown, bushy, white wolves with fur so thick, their heads looked like lions. As we approached their heels, the pack split and we were instantly enclosed by the wolves. It was surreal.

Sitting in a Honda Civic is basically like sitting on a skateboard. The wolves' heads were even with ours and they kept glancing at us with their silver eyes as they ran within three feet of the car. *Creep me out!* I proceeded to do what any civilminded woman would do. I began locking the door locks so the wolves wouldn't get in the car. Rick burst out in a guffaw saying, "Yeah, wolves are known for opening car doors." Not funny.

Our journey in the heat of the pack lasted less than a minute, but it felt like 487 minutes to me. This California girl wasn't accustomed to arctic wolves. Finally, the wolves separated and we began pulling away from the pack. My mind was running amuck, as you can well imagine. I started asking wolf questions: "Do wolves eat people?" Rick was highly reassuring, "Not very often. Only if they're *really* hungry." Good. Relief calmed my soul. He added for his personal amusement, "Those wolves looked *really* hungry." Not funny AGAIN!

My brave husband thought the whole episode was uncommonly cool! I felt like Little Red Riding Hood trapped in a Mutual of Omaha Wild Kingdom show gone bad.

Inside every man God placed the protector gene— translating to 'protect-her.' God designed them to protect and defend. Our role in this whole he-man deal is to let them know they are appreciated. A man will go above and beyond for his wife as long as he knows that she admires him. Pump him up . . . in a healthy, manly way.

MariTaL ADVice x 2

> *Wives, submit to your husbands as to the Lord. For the husband is the head of the wife as Christ is the head of the church, his body, of which he is the Savior. Now as the church submits to Christ, so also wives should submit to their husbands in everything. . . . However, each one of you also must love his wife as he loves himself, and the wife must respect her husband.*
>
> Ephesians 5:22–24, 33

Before choir practice one Sunday morning at church, a young married couple arrived, obviously disgruntled with each other. I pulled the wife aside to see if I could help, and simply to listen if she needed to unload. Their disagreement centered on a new car that she needed, and had picked out, but he had a different car chosen for his bride. We hugged and went our separate ways.

I found a quiet place and wrote her a note explaining that the type of car is nowhere near as important as her submitting to her husband. Sure, she could dig in her heels and get what she wanted, but every time either of them saw the car, they would remember that his wasn't the final word on that purchase. I told her that honoring and respecting her husband was more important than *this* car at *this* moment. It's not easy, but blessing follows obedience, and we are to obey what God wrote in Ephesians. I went on and on for three pages about husbands being hard to figure out, but that we are to honor and love them in spite of themselves.

On our trip home from church that day, Rick told me that he had pulled the young husband aside and heard the same car purchasing problem. I asked Rick what sage advice he delivered. He explained to the husband that women are hard to figure out and the husband's job is to love his wife in spite of that. He encouraged the young man to let his wife choose her car because the type of car was not as important as keeping his wife happy.

I detailed the contents of my letter to Rick and we laughed and laughed. The poor couple was probably having the reverse argument now, "Honey, you pick the car." . . . "No, dear, *you* pick the car."

Weeks later I saw the woman again, and she let me know that she kept my letter in her pocket every day and reread it over and over until it ended up going through the wash. She confided that it wasn't in her nature to give preference to anyone, and she needed a constant reminder. Don't we all?!? The only reason I could write the letter was due to many years of figuring out the truth the hard way. As women we often base our decisions on our feelings, but obedience and submission are acts of the will. Every minute of every day we have to decide to shape our will to do God's will. It's not easy, but it is so freeing.

it all comes out in the wash

> *And we urge you, [sisters], warn those who are idle, encourage the timid, help the weak, be patient with everyone. Make sure that nobody pays back wrong for wrong, but always try to be kind to each other and to everyone else. Be joyful always; pray continually; give thanks in all circumstances, for this is God's will for you in Christ Jesus.*
>
> 1 Thessalonians 5:14–18

Rick and I met at Trinity Western University on the first day of "O" week. First impressions are not always everything, as in our case. The things that impressed Rick and I were not destined to knit us together for all eternity. He was impressed that I was a California girl, and I was impressed that he admitted being from Wildwood. That was the name of the psychiatric hospital not far from our school. Hmmmmm. Come to find out, there is a small town in Alberta also named Wildwood. Rick and I enjoyed several meals together and toward the end of the week Reeko Sauvé showed up at my dorm looking for me. Be still my pulsating heart.

A piece of tan-bark hit my third floor dorm window, and my roommate and I both ran to see who it was. There Rick stood looking like a hobbit from three stories up. I opened the window, all five safety inches that were provided, and said hello. By this time, I was obviously enamored by his black wavy, shoulder length hair, because his first pickup line should have been a bright red flag. Rick yelled, "Hey, Babe, got any laundry detergent?" With eyelashes fluttering, I promised to be right down with the white powdery treasure.

Please tell me what type of guy shows up at college without laundry soap? Or without quarters to buy his own little expensive boxes??? I should have caught on, but I was waist deep in naiveté. I don't recall Rick ever borrowing laundry soap again, but he did continue throwing tan-bark at my window—for the entire year. Was it a presumptuous ploy to spend time with me? Was it a saucy scheme to win my heart? Later that year on "open dorm" Sunday, I visited Rick's room and secretly surveyed his sock and underwear drawer. Everything was neatly folded and in straight rows. Perfect! A girl's got to know these things.

Looking back after 22 years of doing Rick's laundry, I'm convinced that the neat drawer didn't matter at all. I've been tempted once or twice to complain about having to pick up Rick's socks in order to wash them, dry them, fold them and put them away. A friend of mine, who is a single mom, straightened me out real quickly by remarking that she wished she had a husband whose socks she could pick up. Every single time I've picked up a dirty sock since then, I've thanked the Lord that I have a husband. A little laundry perspective was all I needed.

sunglasses and lipstick

> *Your beauty should not come from outward adornment, such as braided hair and the wearing of gold jewelry and fine clothes. Instead, it should be that of your inner self, the unfading beauty of a gentle and quiet spirit, which is of great worth in God's sight. For this is the way the holy women of the past who put their hope in God used to make themselves beautiful.*
>
> 1 Peter 3:3–5

I don't know about you, but I'm OK with not braiding my hair. The last plaits that adorned these locks were fashioned circa 1984. I'm almost OK with not wearing gold jewelry, because, not counting my wedding ring, I switched over to silver jewelry circa 1998. However, I'm not OK skipping the fine clothes. Isn't it interesting how we read passages like this in God's Word? We pick and choose what suits us and our lifestyles, missing the entire gist of what He is trying to convey. Are braids, gold and clothing forbidden? Of course not, but they should not be the essence or the source of our beauty.

I don't know about you, but I Peter 3:4 has caused me some alarm; for never have the words *gentle* and *quiet* been used in a description of me. As you can see with your own eyeballs, this is "of great worth in God's sight." Makes me nervous. How does God view boisterous and determined? What happened to everyone having a part in the Body of Christ? Someone has to be the mouth . . . and what about the funny bone? Come on. When verses in the Bible make me nervous, I look up the main words, hoping for clarification and comfort to my soul. God wouldn't write things to make me uncomfortable, would He?

Gentle: mild, calm, soothing, kindly, considerate, courteous. Well, I scored 3.5 out of 6 on Gentle.

Quiet: peaceful, tranquil, serene, hushed, restrained, modest. I scored just 2 out of 6 on Quiet.

I don't know about you, but I think personality plays a tremendous part in how hard we have to work at behaving like the holy women in the past. My inner self can be very gentle and quiet. It's my outer self that tends to be lively, gritty and animated. Proverbs 16:23 says, "A wise man's heart guides his mouth." *That* is the key. What is in your heart is blatantly obvious by your adornments, vocabulary, body language and attitude.

Proverbs 31:30 says, "Charm is deceptive, and beauty is fleeting; but a woman who fears the LORD is to be praised." I don't know about you, but my goal is to be beautiful by putting my hope in the Lord. You either place your life and family in God's hands, or you don't. It's a mindset, a simple decision. Your beauty depends on it!

If all else fails, take my mother's beauty advice and wear sunglasses and lipstick.

A Woman's Place is in the Laundry Room

> *We have different gifts, according to the grace given us. If a man's gift is prophesying, let him use it in proportion to his faith. If it is serving, let him serve; if it is teaching, let him teach; if it is encouraging, let him encourage; if it is contributing to the needs of others, let him give generously; if it is leadership, let him govern diligently; if it is showing mercy, let him do it cheerfully.*
>
> Romans 12:6–8

Like the dirty cloud that follows Pigpen and his blanket, I could smell the dirt rising as soon as the washing machine broke down. Sitting together in front of the computer as husband and wife, we were reading washing machine reviews. (If you ever have insomnia, I recommend this.) I scanned a review and suggested a model. Rick made several comments, including, but not limited to, "Eighteen cycles! How many did our old washer have?" After a quick jog to the laundry room, I returned and answered, "Twelve." Not surprisingly, he asked, "Why do we need six more? Our clothes were clean with twelve." I explained that the new and improved cycles were for specific washing needs that would be useful and shorter, in order to save money. He didn't get it. The questioning, answering and reasoning went on and on for over an hour. Finally I lovingly inquired, "When you buy an airplane, do you want me sitting beside you asking, 'Ailerons? How many ailerons did your last plane have? Did you use both of them?'" The light bulb went on, thank God. He let me pick out the washing machine all by myself. I figured out that you gotta talk to a pilot in pilot smack. Insert your own husband's occupation as necessary.

Weeks later while busily preparing dinner, I asked Rick if he would throw a load of laundry into our new-fangled LG front loader, which lights up like a cockpit when you hit the magic button. Rick agreed and took the basket of dirty clothes into the laundry room. I heard the basket hit the floor. Next, the door opened. Clothes were loaded and the door was securely fastened for takeoff. Silence prevailed for a long four or five minutes before Rick hollered, "I'm not checked out on this machine." Oh boy. There's only five buttons on the washer. How many are in the cockpit of the million-dollar airplane he flies? Laundry Flight Training commenced immediately.

Selective intelligence is what this is called. I have exercised it myself by refusing to learn how to hook up the DVD player and/or the Wii. Everyone has their own gifting from the Lord, and it usually centers on a task that you love to do or at which you are proficient. I do not love electronics; Rick isn't fond of laundry. By letting each other focus on our "gifts" (term used loosely), Rick doesn't have to wear pink underwear, and I can watch chick flicks to my heart's content. II Timothy 1:6 says, "Therefore I remind you to stir up the gift of God which is in you" (NKJV).

ALL HAIL HOUDINI

> *O LORD, be gracious to us; we long for you. Be our strength every morning, our salvation in time of distress. . . . The LORD is exalted, for he dwells on high; he will fill Zion with justice and righteousness. He will be the sure foundation for your times, a rich store of salvation and wisdom and knowledge; the fear of the LORD is the key to this treasure.*
>
> Isaiah 33:2, 5–6

Long Beach, California was our destination for a romantic, weekend getaway from the blazing temperatures in Phoenix. Half way to our destination we stopped for traveling necessities: gas, snacks and restrooms. We indulged in all three before sauntering back to the car.

Even though Rick is a country boy minus the cowboy boots, he locks everything, including the front door, when retrieving the mail or weeding the front yard. Strangest thing is, as a city girl, I hardly ever lock doors . . . on houses or cars.

I knew our Ford Taurus would be securely locked down upon our return. Safety first. As Rick escorted me to the passenger side, we glanced in the car window and saw his keys dangling from the ignition switch. Realization hit us simultaneously that Safety Man had locked us out.

Rick retrieved a credit card from his wallet, mumbled something about seeing a trick on TV and slid the card between the weather stripping and the car window. I rolled my eyes, but held my tongue, being the supportive wife that I am. To my surprise, he grabbed the door handle and it opened. Impressed! Amazed! Shocked! Elated! I can't quite pinpoint the exact emotion for that moment, but awestruck and thankful were mixed in there too.

A month later I was chattering to Rick about praise-report time at my mom's group, where I recounted his accolades from the saved-by-Rick's-credit-card story. Unexpectedly, he stood up, came over and wrapped his arms around me, pinning my arms to my sides. He whispered in my ear, "I had an extra key for the car in my pocket, and I unlocked your door while I slid the credit card up and down." At that moment, the wrestling hold was a wise decision on his part, to protect him from bodily harm. Under duress I promised Christlike behavior before being released.

Even though some deception and slide-of-hand was involved, for an entire month I was royally impressed with my talented, capable husband. From then on, I have been abashed at my gullibility.

What unlocked the car? A hidden key. As promised in Isaiah, what is the key to a rich store of salvation and wisdom and knowledge for us? The fear of the Lord is the key to this treasure and it's not camouflaged. As dumbfounded as I was by a concealed key, so many times I am flabbergasted why I don't rely on God for the answers to everyday struggles and trials. A sure foundation is accessible to us if we only acknowledge our God in fear and reverence. It truly is that simple. The key is always in our pocket.

A Wife's Alphabet

> *Be clear minded and self-controlled so that you can pray. Above all, love each other deeply, because love covers over a multitude of sins. Offer hospitality to one another without grumbling. Each one should use whatever gift he has received to serve others, faithfully administering God's grace in its various forms.*
>
> 1 Peter 4:7b–10

A Always greet hubby at the door with a kiss.

B Be the best *you*, you can be.

C Cook his favorite meal often.

D Dress up just for him.

E Emphasize his strengths.

F Fun is essential.

G Give him praise.

H Hold his hand whenever possible.

I "I Love You" should be repeated several times a day.

J Joy comes from a thankful heart.

K Know his likes and dislikes.

L Laugh with each other.

m Meet his needs.

n Nurture him body and soul.

o Offer to help him.

p Phone him just to say hello.

q Quickly put arguments to rest.

r Respect and reverence him.

s Say only positive words about him.

t Take an interest in his hobbies.

u Uplift him in prayer.

v Value your time together.

w Whisper sweet nothings in his ear.

x faX a love note to him.

y Your attitude is the example for your home.

z Zip your lip if it's not a positive word.